Culture and
Customs of
Guatemala

Culture and Customs of Guatemala

∽∘∾

Maureen E. Shea

Culture and Customs of Latin America
and the Caribbean
Peter Standish, Series Editor

GREENWOOD PRESS
Westport, Connecticut • London

Library of Congress Cataloging-in-Publication Data

Shea, Maureen E., 1953–
    Culture and customs of Guatemala / Maureen E. Shea.
        p.   cm.—(Culture and customs of Latin America and the Caribbean, ISSN 1521–8856)
    Includes bibliographical references (p.   ) and index.
    ISBN 0–313–30596–X (alk. paper)
        1. Guatemala—Civilization—20th century.   2. Guatemala—Social life and customs—20th
    century.   I. Series.
    F1466.5.S52   2001
    972.8'8105'2—dc21   00–025116

British Library Cataloguing in Publication Data is available.

Library of Congress Catalog Card Number: 00–025116
ISBN: 0–313–30596–X
ISSN: 1521–8856

First published in 2001

Greenwood Press, 88 Post Road West, Westport, CT 06881
An imprint of Greenwood Publishing Group, Inc.
www.greenwood.com

Printed in the United States of America

The paper used in this book complies with the
Permanent Paper Standard issued by the National
Information Standards Organization (Z39.48–1984).

10 9 8 7 6 5 4 3

To my father, James Francis Shea,
who gave me the opportunity to appreciate the rich texture of
Latin American cultures
and who taught me to value the ideals of social justice and solidarity.

And to the memory of my mother,
Regina Fabretto Shea.

Contents

A photo essay follows p. 64.

Series Foreword

"CULTURE" is a problematic word. In everyday language we tend to use it in at least two senses. On the one hand we speak of cultured people and places full of culture, uses that imply a knowledge or presence of certain forms of behavior or of artistic expression that are socially prestigious. In this sense large cities and prosperous people tend to be seen as the most cultured. On the other hand, there is an interpretation of "culture" that is broader and more anthropological; culture in this broader sense refers to whatever traditions, beliefs, customs, and creative activities characterize a given community—in short, it refers to what makes that community different from others. In this second sense, everyone has culture; indeed, it is impossible to be without culture.

The problems associated with the idea of culture have been exacerbated in recent years by two trends: less respectful use of language and a greater blurring of cultural differences. Nowadays, "culture" often means little more than behavior, attitude, or atmosphere. We hear about the culture of the boardroom, of the football team, of the marketplace; there are books with titles like *The Culture of War* by Richard Gabriel (Greenwood, 1990) or *The Culture of Narcissism* by Christopher Lasch (1979). In fact, as Christopher Clausen points out in an article published in the *American Scholar* (Summer 1996), we have gotten ourselves into trouble by using the term so sloppily.

People who study culture generally assume that culture (in the anthropological sense) is learned, not genetically determined. Another general assumption made in these days of multiculturalism has been that cultural differences should be respected rather than put under pressure to change.

But these assumptions, too, have sometimes proved to be problematic. For instance, multiculturalism is a fine ideal, but in practice it is not always easy to reconcile with the beliefs of the very people who advocate it: for example, is female circumcision an issue of human rights or just a different cultural practice?

The blurring of cultural differences is a process that began with the steamship, increased with radio, and is now racing ahead with the Internet. We are becoming globally homogenized. Since the English-speaking world (and the United States in particular) is the dominant force behind this process of homogenization, it behooves us to make efforts to understand the sensibilities of members of other cultures.

This series of books, a contribution toward that greater understanding, deals with the neighbors of the United States, with people who have just as much right to call themselves Americans. What are the historical, institutional, religious, and artistic features that make up the modern culture of such peoples as the Haitians, the Chileans, the Jamaicans, and the Guatemalans? How are their habits and assumptions different from our own? What can we learn from them? As we familiarize ourselves with the ways of other countries, we come to see our own from a new perspective.

Each volume in the series focuses on a single country. With slight variations to accommodate national differences, each begins by outlining the historical, political, ethnic, geographical, and linguistic context, as well as the religious and social customs, and then proceeds to a discussion of a variety of artistic activities, including the press, the media, the cinema, music, literature, and the visual and performing arts. The authors are all intimately acquainted with the countries concerned: some were born or brought up in them, and each has a professional commitment to enhancing the understanding of the culture in question.

We are inclined to suppose that our ways of thinking and behaving are normal. And so they are . . . for us. We all need to realize that ours is only one culture among many, and that it is hard to establish by any rational criteria that ours as a whole is any better (or worse) than any other. As individual members of our immediate community, we know that we must learn to respect our differences from one another. Respect for differences between cultures is no less vital. This is particularly true of the United States, a nation of immigrants, but one that sometimes seems to be bent on destroying variety at home, and, worse still, on having others follow suit. By learning about other people's cultures, we come to understand and respect them; we earn their respect for us; and, not least, we see ourselves in a new light.

Peter Standish
East Carolina University

Acknowledgments

THIS BOOK would not have been possible without institutional support and
the help of various friends and graduate students. I first thank my graduate
research assistants, Scott Cooper, Laura Barbas and especially Marcie Rinka,
for their help, patience and support. I am especially grateful for the warm
friendship of various Maya women, particularly Yolanda, Laura, Magda, Elu-
via and Florentina. From them I learned much about stoic and creative
survival tactics. Special thanks to Ric Finch and Rosa Howard, who gener-
ously provided many of the photos included in this book. Also special appreciation to my craftsman brother, Tom Strain, for his suggestions and
encouragement, and my sister, Regina, who rode "Rebelde" in the highlands
of Guatemala and listened to many long-winded phone calls. And thanks to
the many other New Orleans friends who offered their optimistic cheer and
support; Heidi, Lindas, Christine, Harry, Kathleen, Matthew, Josefa and the
Carrollton Station crowd. For those friends from afar, heartfelt thanks to
Robert Mckenna, who taught me so much about Guatemala and with whom
I shared so much laughter, Janice, for her poetic soul and perceptive observations, Michael, Gay and the Frostburg pack, especially Carol, Johns, James
and Susie. Deep appreciation to George McMurray for his warm encouragement through the years. I am grateful to Barbara for our rich experiences
together in Guatemala, and Guatemalan literary-and-art promoter Max Araujo for introducing me to many of the artists who appear in this book.
Warm appreciation to Jorge Román-Lagunas, organizer of the yearly CILCA
congresses (Congreso Internacional de Literatura Centroamericana), that
have been invaluable in drawing attention to Central American writers, critics

and their works since 1993. Thanks to my brothers, Jim and John, and their families for their support. And a warm thanks to my furry shepherds, Lupo and Salina, who kept my feet warm under the computer many a long night.

I wish to thank the Roger Thayer Stone Center for Latin American Studies at Tulane University for its generous summer research support through grants from the Mellon Foundation. I also thank the Newcomb Foundation, the Newcomb Center for Research on Women, the Graduate School, and the Department of Spanish and Portuguese at Tulane for supporting my research in Guatemala.

Introduction

EVERY COUNTRY in Latin America has distinct cultural characteristics that differentiate it from the others. In Guatemala this uniqueness reveals itself in its ethnic composition. Almost all Guatemalans are descendants of the Mayas and/or Spaniards. However, the majority of the population, between 55 and 65 percent, is Mayan. Second only to Bolivia, Guatemala has the largest population of indigenous people in the Americas. It is important to emphasize that this indigenous identity is mostly an ethnic, and not a racial, category. Most Guatemalans have a mix of Mayan and Spanish blood to varying degrees, with some pure Mayas and a minority of pure-blooded Spanish at either end of the spectrum. So those who consider themselves Maya may have the same racial characteristics as those who do not. A term that is used for the non-Mayan people in Guatemala is Ladino, although such people rarely refer to themselves as Ladinos. Rather, they call themselves Guatemalans.

Basically, whether one is Mayan or Ladino is a question of self-identification. Mayas consider themselves descendants of the ancient Mayas; speak a Mayan language; live in indigenous, rural communities; wear their traditional dress for the most part (although this has changed especially for the men); eat their traditional foods of maize and beans; and generally have an intimate relationship with nature. Ladinos, on the other hand, live mostly in urban centers (although there are Ladino rural villages), dress in European or U.S. clothing, speak Spanish, and commonly reject their Mayan heritage. The following example will make this picture clearer. A Maya may decide for economic, political or other personal reasons that s/he no longer wishes

Map of Guatemala.

to be Mayan. S/he may move away from his or her indigenous community to Guatemala City, learn how to speak Spanish, forget his or her native Mayan language, wear Western rather than Mayan clothing, and learn to eat the fast foods of the city. Therefore this Maya has become Ladino-like, practically indistinguishable from the Ladino masses of the city (s/he occasionally may let slip Mayan words or habits). It can work the other way with a Ladino turning Maya, but this rarely happens since the long history of economic and political discrimination against the Mayas in Guatemala (see Chapter 1) makes it more advantageous to be a Ladino.

This book focuses on Guatemalan cultures and customs, with an emphasis on the fact that there are principally two cultures coexisting in Guatemala, with a minority of African/Caribbean people in its eastern section. It traces the history of the Mayan culture, the advent of the Spaniards and how these distinct worlds went through long periods of acculturation and resistance. It describes how the Mayan and Catholic religions blended and how the world visions of the Maya and the Spanish influenced literature, music, dance, theater, crafts and other arts. Because Mayan life in the highlands has retained a distinctiveness that is unique in all of Latin America, an important part of this book concentrates on the continued existence of Mayan customs and beliefs. As the Mayas have been considered inferior to the Spanish or Ladino population since the arrival of the Spaniards, the issue of ethnic discrimination will appear in discussing the various topics covered. For instance, it is impossible to speak of health-related topics or education without addressing the favored status of the Ladinos.

Because of its beautiful countryside, its temperate climate and the bright colors of Mayan weavings and clothing, Guatemala has been called the land of eternal spring. However, it has been marred by generations of rule by ruthless dictators and by violence that has been directed mostly at the Mayan population. Since the arrival of the Spaniards the main issue in dispute has involved ownership of land. Although Guatemala has moved forward in many ways, this is still the central issue today. For this reason, notwithstanding those sectors of Guatemala that are moving toward a more modernized, progressive and capitalist state, Guatemala still retains its traditional land patterns: a minority of the population owns most of the land while the Indians work those lands for below-subsistence wages. The roots of this situation and what may lie in store in the future will be discussed in the following pages.

Chronology

1523–1524	Pedro de Alvarado arrives to conquer Guatemala for the king of Spain and, in 1524, founds Santiago de los Caballeros, the first Spanish capital in the highlands near present-day Antigua. The site of this capital was changed twice, to what is today known as Ciudad Vieja and then to Antigua.
1528–1530	The Kaqchikel and Quiché Indian tribes unite and rebel against the Spanish but are defeated.
1541	A volcanic eruption destroys the capital.
1543	The Spanish monarchy and the Dominican order establish *reducciones* and force Mayan Indians to abandon their land and relocate.
1681	The University of San Carlos is founded.
1720	King Felipe V abolishes the *encomienda* system.
1773	An earthquake destroys the capital and prompts King Carlos III to move the capital to its present site of Guatemala City.
1821	Guatemala declares independence from Spain.
1823	The Central American Federation is established with Guatemala as its political center. Other territories in the fed-

	eration include the present-day countries of Honduras, El Salvador, Nicaragua and Costa Rica.
1838	José Rafael Carrera overthrows the Central American Federation and establishes himself as the military ruler. His rise to power causes the provinces of the Central American Federation to disband and become separate nations.
1847	Carrera declares Guatemala an independent, sovereign nation.
1859	Carrera fails to get Great Britain to sign a treaty to define the status and boundaries of British Honduras.
1865	Carrera names General Vicente Cerna as his successor.
1871	The Liberals overthrow Cerna and appoint Miguel García Granados as provisional president.
1873	Justo Rufino Barrios overthrows Vicente Cerna and inaugurates a period of liberal government. During his presidency he legalizes civil marriage, secularizes education, expropriates and sells church property, fosters the construction of roads, railways and telegraph lines and opens the country to foreign investment. Barrios erodes Mayan village autonomy by expropriating and selling substantial communal Mayan lands to Ladinos.
1885	Barrios is killed in the Battle of Chalchuapa attempting to reestablish the Central American Federation.
1886	Manuel Lisandro Barillas serves as provisional president for six years.
1892	Justo Rufino Barrios' nephew, José María Reyna Barrios is elected to the presidency.
1898	José María Reyna Barrios is assassinated and Manuel Estrada Cabrera becomes provisional president. Through fraudulent elections, he succeeds himself as president until 1920. Under his tenure, Estrada Cabrera fosters economic development, improves health conditions and stimulates the educational system. Estrada Cabrera is best-known for allowing the Boston-based United Fruit Company to buy land virtually tax free to establish banana plantations.

1920	Estrada Cabrera is declared insane and forced from office by the Unionist Party.
1921	General José María Orellana becomes president.
1926	Lázaro Chacón becomes president.
1931	General Jorge Ubico is elected president.
1934	Ubico passes the Vagrancy Law, which makes workers, especially Mayan Indians, liable for periods of forced labor in service to the government.
1944	The October Revolution, a civilian-military movement, removes the dictator Jorge Ubico and installs a reformist government, eventually led by Juan José Arévalo (1945–1950) and then Jacob Arbenz Guzmán (1950–1954), that establishes a new labor code, creates the National Social Security System, grants suffrage to women and passes agrarian reform. Guatemala continues to enjoy these reforms until 1954. These years are referred to as the "Ten Years of Spring."
1954	Plans for agrarian reform negatively affect the U.S.-owned United Fruit Company. Outraged company leaders accuse President Jacobo Arbenz Guzmán of being a communist. The CIA organizes a military coup. The CIA's Operation Success helps overthrow the democratically elected government of Arbenz, ending a nine-year experiment with democracy. A series of U.S.-supported military dictators rule Guatemala until civilian president Vinicio Cerezo is elected in 1986.
1967	Miguel Angel Asturias wins the Nobel Prize for literature.
1976	An earthquake destroys Guatemala City, killing 30,000, injuring over 70,000 and leaving over 1 million homeless.
1982	Four guerrilla groups join under the banner of the Unidad Revolucionario Nacional Guatemalteco (Guatemalan National Revolutionary Unity, URNG). General José Efraín Ríos Montt takes power after a coup, installs military tribunals and launches a scorched-earth campaign, which is

designed to wipe out guerrilla support in heavily populated Mayan Indian areas. An estimated 626 Mayan Indian villages are destroyed.

1984   The World Council of Indigenous People accuses the Guatemalan military of systematic extermination of indigenous people.

1988   The Guatemalan government officially recognizes the Academia de Lenguas Mayas (Academy of Mayan Languages), one of the most important schools that Mayan intellectuals create to preserve their cultural heritage.

1991   Guatemala abandons its claims of sovereignty over Belize, and the two countries establish diplomatic relations.

1992   Maya activist Rigoberta Menchú Tum wins the Nobel Peace Prize. The government and URNG sign the Accord on Indigenous Rights and Identity.

1996   Alvaro Arzú Irigoyen takes office as new president and continues negotiations with the URNG. A cease-fire in March is followed in September by the signing of a peace accord that officially ends thirty-six years of civil war. The Catholic Church launches the Recuperación Histórica de Memorias (Recovery of Historical Memory project, REHMI).

1998   Bishop Juan Gerardi is murdered in April after publication of the REHMI report.

1999   The United Nations' Historical Clarification Commission publishes a human-rights report that assigns responsibility for the 200,000 deaths of mostly civilians during the 1970s and 1980s to the Guatemalan army and the CIA.

        November 9. Alfonso Portillo, far-right-wing candidate of the Frente Republicano Guatemalteco (Guatemalan Republican Front, FRG), with strong connections to ex-president José Efraín Rios Montt, is elected president of Guatemala.

1

History, Geography and Demographics

PRE-COLUMBIAN MAYAS

BEFORE THE ARRIVAL of the Spanish conquistadors, the area that came to be called Guatemala was populated by numerous Mayan peoples who had lived there for hundreds of years. In fact, the roots of the Mayan civilization may be in the previous civilization of the Olmecs, which was established some 3,000 years ago (Tedlock, 1985). Generally, Mayan civilization is classified into three periods: the Preclassical period, from about 2000 B.C. to A.D. 300; the Classical period, from A.D. 300 to A.D. 900; and the Postclassical period, from A.D. 900 to about A.D. 1500. The Mayans today are remembered and revered largely for the astounding architectural and artistic wonders that they created during the Classical period, which lasted about 600 years. It was during this period that the cities of Tikal, Palenque and Copan flourished. All featured magnificent pyramids and intricate artwork. A long line of royal descendants ruled the cities. The histories of these rulers were inscribed through hieroglyphic writings on various materials, such as paper (bark), pottery and stone—many are still preserved today. Toward the end of the Classical period, it is believed that the populations of these diverse city-states became too numerous to be sustained by the land-based agrarian system, and the Mayan civilization began to disintegrate as people left. The two principal areas that then became centers for Mayan culture and civilization were in northern Yucatán and in the Mayan highlands, especially the area that is known as Quiché. Both of these areas became part of military states that Nahuatl-speaking invaders, perhaps Toltecs from central Mexico, created.

The hieroglyphic writings continued to document the histories of the peoples with a combination of Mayan texts and Toltecan pictures (Tedlock, 1985). Then in the sixteenth century, the Europeans arrived.

It is important to note at this point that the widespread hypotheses about the "disappearance" of the Mayas are fallacies. The Mayas never disappeared. Today there are 4–5 million Mayas living in Guatemala alone (a large number also live in southern Mexico), many of whom practice similar customs and hold the cultural beliefs of their ancestors.

THE ENCOUNTER OF THE EUROPEANS AND MESOAMERICANS

The subsequent history of Guatemala, and the rest of Mesoamerica and Latin America in general, is what has been called—in the recent quincentenary of Christopher Columbus' arrival—an encounter between the European and the Mesoamerican worlds. It led to a long history of turbulence. The Europeans attempted to establish dominance while the Mesoamericans fiercely resisted the invaders, especially initially, although rebellions have continued until the present. It also eventually led to a series of accommodations, made mostly by the indigenous for practical, survival purposes. However, the Europeans consequently found it advantageous to acculturate themselves to the ways of the native population. The Colonial period, lasting for about 300 years, can be described as a time of accomodation, acculturation and resistance.

When Columbus convinced the Spanish monarchs that his expedition to the East Indies would be a worthwhile enterprise, they funded his 1492 trip which would change the face of what came to be the Americas. The Catholic monarchy of Spain, King Ferdinand and Queen Isabella, financed Columbus' trip with the understanding that any new territories discovered or conquered would become personal possessions of the Spanish Crown and that the peoples inhabiting such lands would become their vassals and subjects of the Catholic Church. Columbus died in a Spanish jail many years after his arrival in the Americas, broke, disheartened and still unaware that he had not reached the East Indies but had ventured on territory previously unknown to the Europeans. He had, however, begun a crusade that would bring hundreds of Spanish conquistadors and their armies to conquer territories for the Spanish Crown and to claim souls for the Catholic Church. Hence the expression that the Americas were conquered by and for the sword and the cross.

After the Spaniards under the command of Hernán Cortés entered the Aztec capital of Tenochtitlán and conquered the Aztec empire in 1521, Cortés sent one of his most able and ruthless generals, Pedro de Alvarado, into Central America in 1523. Alvarado eventually entered what came to be Guatemalan territory. With an army of 420 Spaniards and 300 Indians from the Aztec empire, Alvarado took advantage of the war between the Quichés and the Kaqchikeles to form an alliance with the latter and attack the former. In a dramatic battle Alvarado allegedly slew the Quiché leader, Tecúm-Umán, which hastened the defeat of the Quichés. The culminating blow to the Quichés was at Quetzaltenango in 1524, where Alvarado captured and burnt the Quiché leaders to death, then enslaved hundreds of Quichés. Later, with his Kaqchikel allies, he moved to Lake Atitlán to wage war against the Tzutujiles, also defeating them.

THE COLONIAL PERIOD

Having subdued his enemies and rapidly established his dominance in the Kingdom of Guatemala, Alvarado founded the first Spanish capital in the highlands of Guatemala in 1524 near the Kaqchikel capital of Iximché (which means corn in Kaqchikel). However, when Alvarado returned to Spain, where he was named the *adelantado* (governor) of the Kingdom of Guatemala (which consisted of provinces made up of present-day Guatemala, Nicaragua, El Salvador, Costa Rica, Honduras, Belize and Chiapas in southern Mexico), his brother, Jorge de Alvarado, moved the capital to a new site in 1527, today known as Ciudad Vieja, at the base of a towering volcano called Volcán de Agua. Two other volcanoes, Fuego and Acatenango, ringed the area. This was also a region subject to earthquakes and floods. In 1541 a massive eruption devastated the entire city. In 1543 the capital was rebuilt in Antigua, but this and subsequent attempts to rebuild the capital in the same area all ended in disaster. The immense earthquake of 1773 that once again destroyed the city was the definitive factor that motivated King Carlos III to order the transfer of the capital. The governor and the *cabildo* (town council) had also decided that the geologically unstable area was not the best location for a capital city. Over a period of years the capital was moved to a lower area further away from the volcanoes, which is where Guatemala City is today. The site of the old capital is now the famed tourist site of Antigua, Guatemala.

Alvarado's ruthlessness in his treatment of the Indians became legendary. This led to a series of continuing conflicts, first with his former allies, the Kaqchikeles, who rebelled against a heavy tax that Alvarado imposed on them. This time the Quichés and Tzutujiles allied themselves with the Spaniards, who defeated but were not able to subjugate the Kaqchikeles by 1525. Subsequently, the Kaqchikeles and the Quichés united against the Spanish, and war raged between 1528 to 1530 when the principal indigenous leaders were finally defeated, although resistance continued in various forms.

During the next decade the Kingdom of Guatemala was ruled by Alvarado, his brothers, relatives and friends, a style known in Latin America as *personalismo* (based on personal relationships). After Alvarado died in battle in Mexico in 1541 (the same year as the destruction of his capital), the Spanish government created a complex, bureaucratic system to establish more control over its colonies. During the next decades the Spanish settlers used their position of power to enforce their domination over the Indians, initially enslaving them and later imposing the *encomienda* (indentureship) and the *repartimiento* (draft) system of labor on them. The natural tendency of the Indians to live in scattered areas became more marked as many fled into isolated territories to escape their enslaved condition. In 1543 the Dominican friars came up with a plan to consolidate control over the Mayan Indians, thereby making it easier to Christianize them and keep them away from pagan practices. Approved by the Spanish Crown, the colonists forced the Indians to abandon their lands and relocate into *reducciones*, which were villages populated solely by Indians. Although it was initially thought that this would also be a way to protect the Indians from abuse by the Spaniards, the reality was that the *reducciones* facilitated the takeover of the lands by the settlers and the enforcement of the *encomienda* and *repartimiento* systems of forced labor.

The *encomienda* was a grant of Indians that the Spanish Crown awarded to a colonist which was to be used at the discretion of the *encomendero* (landowner). This usually meant that the Indians worked the land of the *encomendero* to pay his tribute, which left them no time to work on their own small parcels of land. Indian women were also forced to be domestic servants, which often involved rape or other sexual relations with the masters. This system of forced indentureship was fraught with abuse and torment of the Indians by the Spaniards, which is why the Spanish Crown unsuccessfully attempted to limit it or abolish it for years. Even though the *encomienda* system was finally abolished in 1720 by King Felipe V, it still continued to exist in practice until some forty years later.

After the middle of the sixteenth century, however, the Spanish Crown ruled that Indians had to be paid for their labor, which lead to a decline in *encomiendas*. Instead, it was replaced by the *repartimiento* system, which was like a much more severe version of a modern-day draft. A percentage of Indian males between sixteen and sixty years of age had to report for work during certain months of the year to fulfill the needs of Spanish officials or individuals. Although the Indians were supposed to be paid a minimum wage and were allowed to return to their villages at the end of the work period, this system was also fraught with all kinds of abuses and was another form of forced labor. All of this contributed to the demise of a large number of Indians. Disease, malnutrition, mistreatment and extreme punishments often resulted in death. Efforts by conscientious clergy were largely ineffectual, and many of them also participated in the abuse.

The result of these policies during the Colonial period was the consolidation of the best lands into the hands of a small number of settlers who had won favor with the Spanish Crown. In addition, Indians were removed from the lands that they had farmed for generations and were then forced into labor for the new landowners. This had immense repercussions concerning Indian and Spanish relations, leading to numerous rebellions and other forms of resistance by the Mayan Indians.

During this period the church played an important role in subduing the Indians, converting them to Christianity and teaching them that they would receive their just reward after death; therefore they should bear the suffering of this life in good faith. Positive measures were undertaken by the clergy, however, to improve the educational system. The first bishop of Guatemala, Francisco Marroquín, founded schools for both Indian and Spanish children as well as training schools for priests. The Dominicans established institutions of higher learning in 1556, and the Jesuits did the same in 1615. The University of San Carlos was founded in 1681; at that time it was limited to pure-blood Spaniards who were devout Catholics. The various orders—Dominicans, Franciscans, Mercedarians, Jesuits and Augustinians—also established orphanages, hospitals and asylums. In turn, the church benefitted both from grants of land that their parishioners donated and from Indian labor on their various projects. In time, the church became known more for its self-serving agenda than for its humane programs.

Many of the Indians who, on the surface, accepted Christianity kept practicing their own religions in secret. As in the rest of Latin America, the eventual result of this would be the emergence of a mixed religion in which characteristics of the Christian and Mayan belief systems merged to create one that included elements of both. Throughout the Colonial period this blending of distinct elements also worked at a racial level. Interracial relations between the Indians and Spanish, whether coerced or chosen, became more and more frequent. For this reason the majority of the population of Guatemala today is of mixed blood, and the distinctions between Indians and non-Indians or Ladinos are more a question of ethnicity than race.

INDEPENDENCE

The Colonial period left a legacy that would determine future relations among Guatemala's mixed population. The majority of Mayan communities were able to survive despite the demographic collapse caused by diseases and violent repression, the loss of most of their lands and, consequently, the slavery or serfdom imposed on them by the Europeans. To protect themselves many Mayas retreated into small, closed communities in the highlands and avoided contact with the Europeans whenever possible. It is thought that these "closed, corporate communities" (Wolf, 1957) may be one of the principal reasons why the Mayan peoples and culture were able to survive the conquest and colonial periods, while in other areas of Latin America entire native populations were exterminated. Meanwhile, the Ladino population— those of Mayan-Spanish blood—felt more and more disenfranchised as class privileges and power were concentrated in the hands of the Spanish of pure blood. Furthermore, the *criollos*, those of Spanish descent who were born in the Americas, were considered inferior to the peninsular-born Spaniards, and they saw their lands and wealth being stripped away by the small minority of Spanish-born colonists.

All of these factors contributed to increasing tensions among Guatemalans at a time that the Spanish Crown was being challenged by the French emperor Napoleon Bonaparte. When Napoleon seized the Spanish throne in 1808 and placed his brother Joseph on it, the Spanish liberals—largely composed of leading *criollo* families—were given a voice in the government and in the creation of the liberal Constitution of 1812. This constitution eliminated some government monopolies and enacted anticlerical reforms. The conservatives—peninsular-born Spaniards and more traditional *criollo* families—forcefully opposed these changes, which threatened their own privileges. This split between the liberals (anticlerical) and conservatives (proclerical) among the propertied elite would influence political developments in Guatemala up through 1944.

When Napoleon was defeated in 1814 and Ferdinand VII was restored to the Spanish throne, the monarch promptly annulled the 1812 Constitution. The new president of the *audiencia* (Spanish colonial court and administration), José de Bustamente, abolished the liberal reforms and established authoritarian rule. However, a process of political participation and debate had been established that fueled the sentiments for independence. In 1820 a revolution in Spain against oppressive rule reestablished the liberal 1812 Constitution and called for freedom of the press, free elections and free trade.

It was in this climate that, in 1821, Colonel Agustín Iturbide turned against the colonial masters and declared the independence of the nascent Mexican empire. By this time both conservatives and liberals in Guatemala had accepted the idea of independence, although their reasons differed. The acting president of the *audienca* of Guatemala, Gabino Gaínza, declared independence in September of 1821, at first allying the country with Mexico. But the Mexican empire became torn apart by internal warring factions, and the Central American Congress declared itself independent in 1823, establishing the Central American Federation. It consisted of the current countries of Guatemala, Honduras, El Salvador, Nicaragua and Costa Rica. The next few years involved the conservatives and liberals jockeying for power. The latter, under the leadership of liberal intellectuals such as Francisco Morazán and Mariano Galvéz, were able to implement significant liberal projects, including the building of schools and roads, the establishment of trial by jury and the abolition of the death penalty (Nyrop, 1983).

However, in 1837 José Rafael Carrera, a twenty-three-year-old illiterate Ladino and religious fanatic, led a rebellion against the liberal governments of the Central American Federation. By claiming that a cholera epidemic that had broken out that year was the consequence of God's displeasure with the anticlerical stance of the liberal government, Carrera gained the support of the conservatives, the Catholic Church, the disenfranchised Ladinos and the Mayas who were spurred on by their priests. With this backing Carrera overthrew the liberal government and took power in Guatemala in 1838. The Central American Federation rapidly disintegrated, and the provinces became separate nations. Carrera then instituted a conservative dictatorial rule in Guatemala that abolished all liberal reforms, strengthened the power of the church and cruelly persecuted those with liberal tendencies. He ruled for twenty-seven years. As president for life he was allowed to pick his successor, another authoritarian conservative, Vicente Cerna, who ruled until 1871. In 1871 the liberals were able to take control of the government under Justo Rufino Barrios, who ruled until 1885. Barrios implemented strong anticlerical measures such as legalizing civil marriages, making education secular rather than religious and, most importantly, expropriating and selling church property (Nyrop, 1983).

Land had come to be recognized as the principal source of wealth in Guatemala. The population, especially the urban and middle classes, was growing. Land became its most coveted resource. In addition, during the Colonial period certain dyes such as indigo (primarily) and cochineal (red dye from the cochineal insect) had been the main export to Europe. As Europeans learned how to make cheaper chemical dyes, it was necessary to seek alternative export crops. Coffee became the export crop of choice, and land was needed to accommodate the large coffee estates. Land was acquired from the church or, again, from the Indians. Although the Mayas had lost the majority of their land, they still retained some, especially on hillsides that the Europeans had deemed undesirable, where they were able to grow their local crops. But because coffee grows well on hillsides, numerous measures were created to dispossess the Mayas of these lands. In addition, harsh peonage laws were established, forcing the Indians to work on the plantations in feudal-like conditions. In short, the Indians became semienslaved to support the export economy, which allowed Barrios to build up Guatemala's infrastructure. He expanded railroad lines and brought electricity, the telephone and the telegraph to the capital. Unemployed Indians were forced to work forty days a year on these projects under newly established vagrancy laws, essentially providing free labor to the government.

Local village authorities were forced to comply with the government and landowners' labor laws. These individuals became viewed as collaborators with the oppressors, creating a climate of suspicion, hatred and resentment in the villages, which did not receive benefits such as electricity. Those local authorities who protested the treatment of their villagers or who resisted the continued expropriation of their lands were treated brutally. In the highland village of Cantel, federal troops killed every local authority in 1884 for resisting the takeover of their lands (Handy, 1984). Various attempts at resistance or rebellion on the part of the Mayas were relatively unsuccessful, as power was consolidated between the Spaniards and Ladinos at the national and local level. Power was thus passed down through the government to the landowners or *caudillos* (strongmen), who ruled by repression. Racial segregation was encouraged. Ladinos, previously also disenfranchised, were considered superior to Indians and came to view themselves as such. They were favored over Indians for any local posts. Formal power was gradually taken away from the peasant Mayan authorities, although it continued to operate on an informal basis through the village elders and the *cofradías* (religious brotherhoods) (Handy, 1984).

After Barrios was killed in battle attempting to reestablish the Central American Federation in 1885, a series of liberal presidents followed, including Barrios' nephew, José María Reyna Barrios. He was assassinated in 1898, and Manuel Estrada Cabrera became president, staying in office illegally until 1920. Estrada Cabrera based his country's economy on Indian labor and foreign investment. It was under him that the Boston-based United Fruit Company was able to acquire extensive plots of land at cheap prices, essentially tax free, to establish banana plantations on which the Indians were forced to work at slave wages. Landowners and local officials ensured that the peonage system continued to operate, and those who protested were incarcerated or assassinated. Increasingly repressive, cruel, corrupt and mentally unbalanced, Estrada Cabrera gained the enmity of various sectors. Several attempts were made to assassinate him. He was finally overthrown in 1920.

During the 1920s Guatemala was ruled by General José María Orellana (1921–1926) and then by Lázaro Chacón (1926–1930). Although some liberal reforms took place, they facilitated the United Fruit Company's takeover of huge tracts of lands. Opposition to the growing monopoly by Guatemalans was silenced. Chacón's rule ended when he suffered a crippling stroke in 1930. At the same time the world plunged into a dark era of economic and political disaster.

It is important to note that despite their progressive legislation, the liberals did not concern themselves with the plight of the Indians. The Mayas were viewed as ignorant, lazy and incompetent peasants, a blight to the country. Nineteenth-century positivist racial theories, in which dark-skinned races were considered naturally inferior to whites, persisted. As such it was thought that the best that could be done to encourage the economic development of the country was to use the Indians as free labor, which was considered somewhat better than the more radical views that espoused the extermination of the Indians. In any event, the needs of the majority Indian population were ignored while an elite Spaniard or near-Spaniard minority flourished. This led to a series of frustrated rebellions by Mayan Indians, who were periodically forced to leave their communities and land to work on the estates of the large landowners. It is necessary to point out that the voting population was a minority and that presidents were elected by an extremely small, educated percentage of the male population. This disenfranchised the Mayas and a majority of the Ladinos and women.

In 1931 Jorge Ubico was elected president of Guatemala. He ruled with an iron hand for thirteen years, tolerating no dissent. Ubico ran his government with an emphasis on honesty and fiscal reform. He was able to bolster an economy on the verge of collapse by granting favorable conditions to foreign investors, and by exploiting the Indians as a labor force. Although he abolished the debt peonage system that had kept the Mayas living in semifeudal conditions, he introduced a severe vagrancy law. This law required Indians to carry a passbook that proved that they had worked 100 to 150 days a year on the large estates of the elite or on the many public projects that Ubico implemented. If the Indians could not prove this, they were jailed or worse. In some ways Ubico weakened the feudal dominance of landowners over the Mayas by abolishing the peonage system. However, it is apparent that he was not concerned with the situation of the Indians. He thought that they were inferior, and he consistently backed the landowners' demands for more labor or land. He also removed the authority of the local Mayan mayors by appointing an *intendente* (administrator), usually from Guatemala City, who reported directly to him. This was another way of eroding local Indian autonomy and establishing the dominance of the Ladinos.

Ubico was a paranoid man obsessed with the military. He admired the fascists and saw himself as a self-styled Napoleon, surrounding himself with pictures of the emperor (Handy, 1984). He imagined conspiracies everywhere. He was heavily guarded and had an extensive network of spies and informants to keep him alerted to all kinds of matters, such as any inefficiency in the state bureaucracy. Thousands of state employees who made mistakes lost their jobs, and some lost their lives. He imposed severe censorship of the press. Murmurs of dissension led to the incarceration and murder of thousands of people who protested his undemocratic rule, among them students, professors, labor organizers and civilian politicians.

A crucial element of Ubico's economic plan was to cultivate foreign investors, which initially included various European countries. Gradually, however, Ubico found himself granting more and more favorable terms to the United States, principally to gain U.S. support for his illegal, fixed reelections. By 1940, 90 percent of Guatemalan produce was being sold to the United States (Handy, 1984). Prior to that, German coffee growers had controlled most of the coffee production in Guatemala. Although Ubico admired the German fascists, to gain favors from the United States he expropriated German territories in Guatemala and expelled many Germans to internment camps in Texas and North Carolina in the early 1940s. At the same time he allowed the United Fruit Company to exploit the Indian labor force. He also granted the company exemptions from import duties and property taxes, and he allowed a branch of United Fruit, the International Railways of Central America, to establish an extensive network that included a railroad, a radio and telegraph company, a port and a shipping line. The result of Ubico's policies was weakened economic ties with other countries and consolidated U.S. economic and political dominance in the region.

Ironically, Ubico's close adherence to the Allies during World War II brought attention to their ideals of freedom, which gained widespread support among educated Guatemalans. His dictatorial, repressive governance style was contrary to the progressive, humanitarian programs of the Allies. With such a foreign model to follow, university students, especially, and other activists increasingly resisted Ubico's brutal repression. Student and labor demonstrations and revolts grew as Ubico became more and more repressive.

After a major strike called the *huelga de brazos caidos* (the strike of the limp arms) during the October Revolution, Ubico was forced to resign in 1944. He was at the time one of the largest landowners in Guatemala.

THE TEN YEARS OF SPRING: 1944–1954

After Ubico's resignation and the resulting turmoil, a three-man junta composed of two military officers, Major Javier Arana and Captain Jacobo Arbenz Guzmán, and one civilian, Jorge Toriello, ruled as a provisional government for two years. They governed until 1945 when they handed over the presidency to a progressive and democratic intellectual, Juan José Arévalo, who was elected largely because of widespread, enthusiastic student support. The 1945 Constitution indicated the new direction that the country was to take. Although the rights of the individual were important, collective interests were more vital. The disenfranchised majorities were to be included in the new program of moving the nation forward into a modern, capitalist economy. One of the first steps was the granting of voting privileges to illiterate males, who were mostly Mayan Indians, and to literate females. However, this latter step left out three-fourths of women and just about all Mayan women. The military was charged with enforcing the constitution and ordered to stay out of politics. Arévalo also implemented various health reforms, establishing clinics in rural Indian villages, providing potable water and installing sewers. He established social security and greatly expanded educational opportunities, promoting literacy throughout the rural areas. He granted labor unions extensive rights, setting minimum wages and limiting child and female labor. Despite these important reforms, however, Arévalo was not able to achieve widespread structural change because he did not attempt to implement the most controversial change: land reform. For this reason he was able to hold onto his fragile grip on the presidency. It was left to his successor, Captain Jacobo Arbenz Guzmán, to attempt to change the feudal system that the large landowners and foreign interests controlled.

Arbenz Guzmán won the 1950 election due to overwhelming support among the masses, including peasants, students, labor and left-wing groups. He did much to encourage their continued participation in the government's policy decisions. To allow Guatemala some economic independence and to better the lot of the Indian peasants in the highlands, he attempted to diversify crop production and establish alternative institutions to compete with those that United Fruit dominated. The central and most controversial aspect of his program, land reform, became law in 1952. Because it was responsible for the overthrow of Arbenz Guzmán, and because it has been looked upon nostalgically as the moment during which Guatemala might have taken a different turn, it is worth examining.

Far from being a communist measure, as Guatemalan landowners, conservatives and U.S. businesses decried it, the Law of Agrarian Reform was a progressive measure intended to redistribute unused or underutilized land to the landless Indian peasants, to give them an opportunity to better their lives and their community and to participate in the national economy. Lands that were to be redistributed were public lands, those that were not farmed or those in excess of 488 acres, with exceptions made for those that were efficiently farmed. All of those who received land had to pay the state a certain percentage of the profits from their crops, from 3 to 5 percent. Some would eventually hold ownership after twenty-five years. Others would relinquish ownership upon death of the primary holder, and that land would return to the state. The state would compensate expropriated land with government bonds holding interest. The most controversial aspect of the law was that the value of property would be compensated in accordance with what had been reported for tax purposes. Because it was a traditional practice to underrepresent the full value of the lands, the landowners considered this an attack on their assets. Furthermore, the landowners were not allowed to protest the law through violent means or their properties could be confiscated, a measure that the Arbenz Guzmán government took to ensure that the law would be implemented. Other aspects of the law angered the large landowners, who claimed violations of their individual and constitutional rights. However, any agrarian reform would have run into these obstacles because Arbenz Guzmán was, in fact, attacking the very basis of the wealth of the elite landowners, many of whom belonged to families that had held power since the invasion of the Europeans.

On top of this, the United Fruit Company perceived the measure as an attack on their powerful empire. As only 15 percent of their land was utilized, the agrarian reform directly threatened their holdings, as the underutilized land was subject to expropriation to be turned over to peasants. Although Arbenz Guzmán did not attempt to directly nationalize the company and take over the territories, he implemented a series of measures that infuriated United Fruit, which had been backed by previous Guatemalan presidents and the U.S. government. The company was accustomed to doing as it pleased. The Board of Directors of United Fruit was especially angered by the provision that the value of their land would be determined by what they had reported for tax purposes, since they had misrepresented this value for years. Finally, they were infuriated when Arbenz Guzmán demanded that the International Railway Company, a branch of United Fruit, pay $10.5 million in back taxes.

The result of the Law of Agrarian reform was vast but short-lived. By 1954, when Arbenz Guzmán was overthrown by a CIA-led military coup, more than 100,000 landless peasants, mostly Indians, had received land to farm. In addition, wages had increased among those peasants who did not receive land as the labor pool dwindled and landowners had to compete for workers, access to government-controlled credit had freed many peasants from the informally practiced peonage system, and the harvest had been bountiful as the underutilized land was put into production. But powerful forces had been alienated. United Fruit began a campaign in the United States to label the Guatemalan government as communist. In the McCarthy era of yellow journalism, a frenzy took hold of the U.S. press, creating near hysteria about the communist regime in its own backyard. Under the Eisenhower administration, with John Foster Dulles as secretary of state and his brother, Allen Dulles, as head of the CIA, antagonism grew. Arbenz Guzmán refused to compromise his agrarian reforms despite increasing pressure from a series of U.S. ambassadors to Guatemala. Both of the Dulleses had close ties to the United Fruit Company, and they convinced Eisenhower that the company was being victimized by the communist regime in Guatemala. At the time a small group of communists was active in Guatemala, with Arbenz Guzmán allowing them the freedom of speech that any other political party had; this did not alleviate the situation. The Catholic Church, long an ally of the landowners and the conservatives who defended the power of the clergy, also joined in the hue and cry about the communist agrarian reforms which threatened their own properties. In short, the landowners, the Catholic Church, the United Fruit Company, and the U.S. government formed a powerful alliance and began to pressure the military, which had backed Arbenz Guzmán's reforms for the most part, to abandon its president. Finally, the CIA launched Operation Success in 1954 to overthrow Arbenz Guzmán. Airplanes strafed Guatemala City as part of a CIA-backed invasion led by its puppet, former Guatemala-military colonel Carlos Castillo Armas. Informed that the Guatemalan military would not defend his presidency, Arbenz Guzmán resigned. Castillo Armas' invading force entered Guatemala City, and through various farcical shenanigans he became president. He annulled the 1945 Constitution, did away with the Law of Agrarian Reform and returned the expropriated lands. Under the new constitution only literate people were allowed to vote, which disenfranchised almost all Indians and most women. Left-wing political parties were made illegal, and numerous peasant organizers and labor leaders were executed without trial. As various scholars have put it since, it was a tragic end to a period of hope in which Guatemala might have escaped its feudal history and entered into a modern, capitalist, egalitarian, democratic society. Instead, the end of this period left the Indians marginalized without a voice or a vote, ensured Ladino dominance, and reestablished class and race privileges for the minority elite. In the subsequent decades the army consolidated its power and ruled intermittently through various military dictators until the 1980s.

THE ERA OF DARKNESS

After the overthrow of Arbenz Guzmán, a small group of Ladino urban rebels formed in the eastern area of Guatemala to resist the military regimes that followed. Originally organized and led by marginalized Ladino leftist intellectuals with little interest in establishing connections with the indigenous population, this nascent revolutionary movement was eradicated in the late 1960s. It resurfaced in the early 1970s in the predominantly Mayan-populated western highlands. Army repression intensified against not only the guerrillas but also against "potential subversives," a classification that included any Maya living in or nearby an area of guerrilla activity. In reaction to attacks by the army, Mayan participation in the guerrilla movement grew. The army, fueled by reports of subversive communist groups, adopted the scorched-earth technique that U.S. troops practiced in Vietnam. This involved the destruction of villages, people and land to ensure that a support network for the guerrillas was not viable. In 1984 the Guatemalan military bragged that it had eliminated 440 Mayan villages in the highlands (although in February 1999, the Historical Clarification Commission documented 626 cases). The tragedy behind this tale is immense. Although it is impossible to estimate accurately, about 100,000 Mayan Indians lost their lives through torture, mutilation and execution at the hands of the military. Countless Mayan women and girls were raped and murdered, and hundreds of thousands of Mayas fled into the mountains and jungles or into exile in Mexico. It has been estimated that 1 million Mayas live displaced in Mexico or in their own country. Initially, few of these had anything to do with the guerrillas.

What this tells us about Guatemalan history is that despite the efforts of progressive-minded leaders and visionary intellectuals who understood that the Mayas were Guatemalans and should be treated as other Guatemalans are, most Spanish or Ladino conservatives and military leaders who controlled policy decisions still persisted in their nineteenth-century views that the Mayas were racially inferior and a blight to the country. Burning entire villages and massacring their inhabitants were justified not only to prevent possible support for the guerrillas but also because the Maya were dispensable, much as animals are. Indeed, some have seen the army's practices as an attempt, once and for all, to exterminate the Mayas and become a modern, non-Indian state. What happened during these decades has been called genocide perpetuated by the Guatemalan military. An entire race of people was automatically condemned for their indigenous identity.

Ricardo Falla, a Guatemalan Jesuit activist, has described this period of violent history that culminated in the massacres of 1982–1983 as a time when "blood flowed like water with the military regimes of General Lucas García and General Efraín Ríos Montt" (Falla, 1992). Rigoberta Menchú, a Quiché woman who survived despite the deaths of many of her family members, details what happens to her and her community during the 1970s in her testimony given to Venezuelan-born anthropologist Elisabeth Burgos in the famous book *Me llamo Rigoberta Menchú y así me nació la conciencia*, translated into English as *I, Rigoberta Menchú* (see Chapter 6).

Meanwhile, on an urban level, vigilante groups had mushroomed to rid Guatemala of what they considered "communist subversives." These "subversives" included anyone who voiced opposition to government policies, such as students, professors, civilian politicians, labor organizers, the opposition press and so on. The Mano Blanco (White Hand) and Ojo por Ojo (An Eye for an Eye) carried out their torture, mutilations and murders supposedly independent from the government and the military. But it is clear that they worked with the hidden consent of these institutions, the national police and even the hierarchy of the Catholic Church. Thousands of people who spoke out against increasingly repressive measures by the military rulers lost their lives or were "disappeared" by these vigilante groups, never to be seen or heard from again. Left-wing groups retaliated by kidnapping and executing several prominent political figures of the Right, but on a minor scale.

The 1970s were a time of terror for most Guatemalans. Ruled first by Carlos Arana Osorio (1970–1974), who controlled the right-wing death squads, then by the somewhat moderate Kjell Eugenio Langerud García (1974–1978), and finally by the ruthless Romeo Lucas García (1978–1982) and José Efraín Ríos Montt (1982–1983), repression grew to intolerable measures. Bodies appeared almost weekly on the campus of the University of San Carlos. As the center for intellectual development and free thinking, the university had become the focus for protests and the denunciation of human-rights violations. As a result, the death squads sought to squash this resistance by kidnapping victims, often students, and leaving their mutilated bodies on the campus.

Then the 1976 earthquake struck Guatemala. This was a major quake that hit most of Guatemala, but it affected mainly the poor in their gingerly constructed cane or cardboard dwellings. About 30,000 people died, 70,000 were injured, and over a million were left homeless. Many foreign countries, including the United States, sent generous amounts of foreign aid. Although Arana Osorio wanted to emulate the example of dictator Anastasio Somoza in neighboring Nicaragua, who had stolen much of the aid sent to his devastated country after an equally severe earthquake, the Guatemalan dictator had discredited himself enough and was not able to gain a hold of the foreign dollars. However, the aftershocks of the quake increased social tensions, as the most affected segments of the population found themselves in even worse situations. Meanwhile a new guerrilla group called the Ejército Guerrillero de la Pobres (Guerrilla Army of the Poor, EGP) had appeared in the area of Quiché in 1972. In 1979 another guerrilla group, Organización del Pueblo en Armas (Organization of People in Arms, ORPA), became active. The military's counterinsurgency tactics were extreme, leading to the indiscrimate murder of Mayan men, women, and children, who were mostly peaceful peasants attempting to eke out a meager existence.

It was at this time that human-rights reports began to appear in the United States about the rampant kidnapping and murdering of thousands of civilians. This caused the U.S. government to issue a warning to the Guatemalan government, which reacted angrily. The result was that the U.S. government, pressured by human-rights organizations, cut off military aid to Guatemala until 1983.

Under Lucas García the political and economic situation worsened. Repression increased and the economy suffered as the majority of the wealth remained frozen in the hands of the elite. Tourism, an important source of revenue, became scarce as human-rights violations became public knowledge. Army officers were also increasingly unhappy under Lucas García, blaming their lack of success in defeating the guerrillas to inefficiency among the top command. They finally overthrew Lucas García in 1982, and General José Efraín Ríos Montt became president.

Ríos Montt did nothing to improve the human-rights record of the Guatemalan presidency. As an ardent Evangelical, however, he used his position to undermine the power of the Catholic Church and champion the conversion of thousands of Mayas to the Evangelical faith. Many Mayas did so, believing that they would be less victimized if they belonged to the same faith as the president. Others converted because some of the basic practices were appealing to them. Mayan women, especially, appreciated that the Evangelical sects did not allow alcohol consumption, a problem that had become severe among landless Mayan men. Also, at that time the Catholic Church had been influenced by a new way of thinking called liberation theology, which professed that the church had an obligation to assist its parishioners by protecting them against repression and violence and searching out means for social justice. Although the hierarchy of the Catholic Church remained staunchly conservative, many young priests, nuns, and lay workers in the highlands worked to educate the Indians and empower them against the forces of oppression. As a result, those Mayas associated with the Catholic Church were more quickly targeted as subversives and eliminated than members of the Evangelical sects were. This eventually started a movement that would have tremendous influence in Mayan villages. People became divided between Catholicism and Evangelicalism. In the early 1990s it was estimated that about 35 percent of this traditionally Catholic country had converted to Evangelicalism.

The guerrilla groups operating in the highlands initially had little Indian support. But as brutal military attacks on villages grew, many peasants began to flee their homes. In 1978 various grassroots organizations united to form the Comite dé Unidad Campesina (United Peasants Committee, CUC). The CUC attempted non-violent measures of resistance with generally tragic results. A well-known effort was the march from the highlands to the capital by a group of Mayas from Quiché representing the CUC in 1980. Along with student and other grassroots supporters, they occupied the Spanish embassy in Guatemala City to publicize the army atrocities that were taking place in their villages. One of the leaders was Vicente Menchú, father of Rigoberta Menchú, the 1992 Nobel Peace Prize laureate. He, along with thirty-eight other peasants and supporters, were burnt to death inside the embassy after army forces attacked and set fire to the embassy, despite protests by the Spanish ambassador. One peasant survived, badly burnt, and was later abducted from the hospital and murdered. As a result, the Spanish government broke off diplomatic relations with Guatemala. After numerous similar episodes, many Mayas began to see no recourse but to join the guerrillas and resist army brutality, although many more attempted to resist taking sides in a conflict that they believed had little to do with them as Mayas.

Violence against the Mayas in the highlands increased under the reign of Ríos Montt. Human-rights agencies such as Americas Watch (1982) and Amnesty International (1981) estimated that by the end of 1982 at least 50,000 people were killed, over 200,000 refugees had fled to Mexico, with another million hiding in the hillsides and jungles or relocating to the slums of Guatemala City. The military responded by instituting a series of measures to consolidate their control over the rural areas and diminish any potential support for the guerrillas. One measure was the creation of model villages, which entailed rounding up terrified Indians in the highlands and relocating them into villages that the military had created. There they were drilled on the evils of communism and the virtues of the Guatemalan military until they professed to believe their lecturers. Another measure involved setting up army garrisons in major villages and forcing surrounding villagers to relocate to what was called a strategic hamlet. In this way the army could keep an eye on the villagers and make sure that they had no contact with the guerrillas. To further ensure its control, the army also set up civil patrols. Virtually all village males, from the ages of sixteen to sixty years, were forced to participate in patrolling their villages and surrounding areas in search of subversives, who could be anybody. This also meant that they were supposed to report any suspicious activities in the villages, such as the gathering of more than three people at a time. If a member of the civil patrols did not report such activities, he paid dearly, many times through torture or death. At times, if a member of the military suspected that a villager was not pro-military, relatives were forced to accuse him or her. This led to the further fracturing of traditional village ties because civil-patrol members could use their positions to avenge themselves against their local enemies. Finally, the army attempted to improve its image by supplying some food and medicine and by helping to reconstruct villages. However, this was also a way to make the Indians, not allowed to travel the distance to farm their plots of land, economically dependent on the military. International opinion continued to condemn the Guatemalan military for its human-rights abuses, and the U.S. government refused to contribute economic or military aid despite then-President Reagan's attempts to convince Congress to do so.

Ríos Montt's regime lasted only eighteen months, but it left a profound imprint on the Guatemalan highland communities. Ríos Montt removed the mayors from hundreds of villages and appointed his own, who reported directly to him. This further destroyed local autonomy and traditional structures of governance. The army established its control over the Indian villages and worked to undermine the centuries-old traditions and customs of the native culture. Fundamentalist preachers mushroomed throughout the countryside and attempted to "modernize," that is, "de-Indianize" the Mayas, convincing them that their economic well-being was better served by becoming more Ladino-like. One may speculate that Mayan culture was, and is today, at more of a precarious point than it has been since the arrival of the Europeans almost 500 years ago. However, there have been important changes that may open a new chapter in a country with such a violent and tragic history.

One important change was the election of Vinicio Cerezo, a civilian president, in 1986. He and his civilian successors have been somewhat ineffectual in reforming a system that caters almost entirely to the elite one percent of the population in league with the still-dominant military leadership. However, that the military permitted the election of a civilian president demonstrates an acknowledgment, at least by some factions of the army, that it has made grave mistakes and needs to improve its record if the country is to evolve into a more modern, capitalist society. International opinion has also had an impact, as foreign aid has been tied to the Guatemalan human-rights record. Ladinos and Mayas are beginning to understand that to better their lot they need to set aside their ethnic differences and work together to create better social, economic and political terms for themselves. Mayan intellectuals, in particular, have founded various schools and academies whose curriculum places an emphasis on the importance of their cultural heritage. Perhaps the most important is the Academia de Lenguas Mayas de Guatemala (Academy of Mayan Languages of Guatemala), which the government formally recognized in 1988. In acknowledging the existence of twenty-one separate Mayan language groups, the government for the first time technically recognized the existence of Mayan culture. The academy is part of the Consejo de Organizaciones Mayas de Guatemala (the Council for Mayan Organizations of Guatemala), an umbrella organization that consists of nineteen other groups working on Mayan cultural questions. Peasant organizers, guerrillas and Catholic activists have all worked to improve the lot of the peasants in the highlands. They, along with the moderate elements of the government and military, were able to hammer out a peace accord that was signed in December 1996.

However, Guatemala still has a long road to pave. Paramilitary violence continues in the form of mostly right-wing death squads. Unemployed soldiers resort to crime and violence. Hundreds of thousands of Mayas still live in abominable conditions in refugee camps, or in extreme poverty and poor health in their homelands. Poor Ladinos and displaced Mayas live in miserable conditions in Guatemala City and other major cities. And student activists, teachers, labor organizers and Catholic priests and nuns continue to be persecuted for speaking out. The main factor that could mean real change in this harsh land, which the civilian presidents do not dare to address, is, once again, land reform. Until there are extensive agrarian reforms enacted, Guatemala will continue its semifeudal structure with little possibility of improving the living conditions of millions of Indian and non-Indian Guatemalans.

DEMOGRAPHY AND ETHNICITY

Upon the arrival of the Europeans in 1492, it is estimated that the population of Central America consisted of 8 million inhabitants. This number rapidly diminished as the wars between the natives and the Europeans intensified. Although the natives had the advantage in numbers, the Spaniards had far superior weapons, such as cannons that killed many people at once. The Spaniards terrorized and disseminated entire native populations. However, the major factor in the demographic collapse of the Americas was the diseases that the Europeans brought to which the natives had little resistance. Hundreds of thousands died of epidemics such as smallpox and pulmonary illnesses. Some native populations came close to extinction, especially in the Antilles. In Central America it is estimated that one-third to one-half of the population perished (Macleod, 1973).

After the initial encounter in Guatemala, many Mayas secluded themselves in the highlands and attempted to avoid contact with the Europeans. In this way they established a centuries-long tradition of protecting themselves and their culture from the invaders. Principally for this reason the Mayas maintained a cultural autonomy that allowed them to live much like their ancestors did. They practiced the same customs and traditions, respected the same communal laws, cultivated the same crops of maize and beans, spoke the same Mayan languages and wore the same ethnic dress of their ancestors. Meanwhile, the Spaniards established their cultural traditions in the capital cities, first in Antigua and then in Guatemala City, which extended into the coastal areas. This is why the western Guatemalan highlands are associated with Mayan culture and have more in common with the Mayan areas of southern Mexico, while the eastern highlands and coastal areas have a majority population and cultural traditions of non-Indians. This area is culturally more similar to El Salvador and Honduras.

The population of Guatemala consists of about 10 million people. It is estimated that about 55 to 60 percent are Mayas, about 40 to 45 percent are Ladinos, and about 4 percent are Black Caribs or Garífuna (African/Caribbean people). (The distinction between Mayas and Ladinos is clarified in the Introduction.)

An accurate census is difficult due to the widely dispersed population in remote, rural areas and some citizens' justifiable fear that census information would be used for draft, tax or other purposes. It is the only country in Central America that is still largely Indian, and it retains much of the linguistic and other cultural manifestations of the Mayas. It is second in Latin

America only to Bolivia in its Indian population. This has given Guatemala a unique, rich cultural tradition.

Language is an extremely important cultural marker for the Mayas. There are twenty-one recognized Mayan languages and various unofficial ones spoken in Guatemala. The most widely spoken languages are Quiché, Kaqchikel, Mam and Kiché. The recent attempts to eradicate the Mayas and their culture has made the use of Mayan languages even more significant in preserving their culture. Many Mayas today are fluent in their native language and Spanish, as Spanish is used for all state purposes. Efforts to promote bilingual schooling have helped. However, in more remote areas, some Mayas remain monolingual. Traditionally, Mayan men who participate in public life are bilingual, while Mayan women who remain in the home are monolingual. However, this is changing due to shifting gender roles (see Chapter 3).

GEOGRAPHY

Despite Guatemala's modest size—its territory consists of 42,000 square miles—it is the most populated country in Central America.

Guatemala contains three natural areas. The largest, which encompasses nearly half of Guatemala, is the lowland area of the north. This includes the Petén, the Caribbean littoral near Lake Izábal, and a stretch that runs through northern Huehuetenango to Alta Verapaz, now known as the Franja Transversal del Norte. It is a sparsely populated region, consisting of a diverse population of Indians and Ladinos. Black Caribs and recent Jamaican migrants live mostly in the Caribbean stretch. The Bay of Amatique on the Caribbean houses the ports of Puerto Barrios, Livingston and Santo Tomás de Castillo. Most of the land is covered by tropical rain forest, and has a hot and humid climate. Plantations that grow bananas and coffee have been established in the inland valleys.

Stretching into Mexico's Yucatán peninsula, with Belize bordering the east, is the immense area of the Petén. This constitutes one-third of Guatemala's area. Because its tropical climate is punctuated by a short dry season, it has been classified as quasi-rain forest. It is in this area that the Classical Maya established their city-states, which flourished for 600 years (A.D. 300–900). It is the site of the famous ruins of Tikal, which has numerous immense and awe-inspiring pyramids as well as ancient sculptures and stelas with engraved Mayan hieroglyphics. It is also home to a variety of wildlife, including spider monkeys, howler monkeys, toucans, foxes, deer, boars, jaguars and a variety of birds.

A second natural area consists of the highlands of Guatemala, which are composed of mountain ranges with numerous volcanoes traversing the region from east to west. There are thirty-three volcano peaks on the southern side, many of which are still active. The major mountain range, the Sierra Madre, runs parallel to the Pacific coastline from Mexico to El Salvador and contains fourteen major volcanoes. The highlands hold more than half of the rural population, which is divided into the *occidente* (western) region, with mostly a Mayan population, and the *oriente* (eastern) region, which is largely populated with Ladinos. A third natural area is a narrow lowland stretch of Pacific coastline.

The natural environment of the western highlands, and the culture and traditions of its Mayan inhabitants, are more similar to the Mayan region of southern Mexico than to the rest of Guatemala. The eastern area of Guatemala, especially the coastal region, is dominated by Ladinos, who have more in common with the Ladino populations of El Salvador and Honduras.

Guatemala City is in a mountain valley that divides the western and eastern highlands. Guatemala City contains a bustling population of about 1 million residents. The population has increased in recent years as more and more rural peasants flock to the shanty towns on the outskirts, especially those Mayas displaced from the highlands by the violence of the 1970s and 1980s. The city suffered two major earthquakes, one in 1917–18. An even more severe earthquake that killed about 30,000 people hit in 1976, especially affecting those living in impoverished areas of flimsy, makeshift dwellings.

In various sections of Guatemala City's commercial zones, the sidewalks in front of all kinds of businesses are packed with vendors selling their wares to throngs of pedestrians under a myriad of low-hanging billboards that sometimes block out the sky. The streets are clogged with cars, trucks, crowded public busses and taxis, many of which emit noxious fumes that contribute to a severe pollution problem. The residential areas for the well-off are spacious and peaceful, with tree-lined avenues, large parks and attractive buildings. In the center of the city lies the Parque Central, which is bordered by the Cathedral, the National Palace and the National Library. The city has numerous museums and cultural centers. It is decorated by engrossing sculptures and paintings by contemporary Guatemalan artists (see Chapter 8). The intellectual elite of the city participate in invigorating *tertulias* (informal discussions about literature, the arts and so on), which seemingly contradict the cloud of censorship that hangs over the more controversial writers and artists. An increasing number of Mayan artists and writers contribute to the dynamic intercultural exchange that takes place at the universities and other linguistic, literary or artistic milieus. There are numerous restaurants, bars and nightclubs where one may hear a variety of music, ranging from local marimba bands and popular musicians to New Orleans jazz or Jamaican reggae.

Guatemala City's shanty towns are largely made up of the most impoverished Ladinos and the many displaced Mayan Indians who migrate to the city. The inhabitants generally live in desperate conditions. They suffer from severe malnutrition, sicknesses and diseases that are caused by a lack of potable water, sanitation and wholesome foods. Although some are lucky enough to find minimally paying jobs in the city and eventually move out, most are abused and discriminated against by the upper classes. Many find their situations worsening. Violence is common. Street gangs, many made up of children, stem from these areas. There are also thieves and beggars of all varieties.

About fifteen miles west of Guatemala City lies Antigua, the former capital. Surrounded by majestic volcanoes, it is a beautiful, small city of colonial-style structures and modern, tasteful buildings. Narrow cobblestone streets and even narrower sidewalks wind through the city. In the center of town lies the main plaza, the Parque Central, which on weekends and market days is surrounded by energetic, skillful Mayan artisans and vendors who travel from nearby Indian villages. There are also the inevitable throngs of tourists. Numerous, permanent, open-air artisan marketplaces currently exist as well as a variety of indoor stores selling Mayan goods. The town has an abundance of ancient churches, monasteries and convents that stem from the sixteenth century, although they are difficult to date as the stalwart, thick structures built to resist earthquakes resemble architectural designs from earlier periods. The main Cathedral on the Parque Central is believed to contain the remains of Pedro de Alvarado, the Spanish conqueror. Nearby, one may view the ruins of the home of Bernal Díaz del Castillo, the soldier who wrote one of the most famous chronicles of the conquest in the sixteenth century. Antigua is known for its foreign-language schools, over fifty of which offer Spanish instruction on a one-to-one or group basis. This, besides the predominance of Mayan culture, is a main attraction for tourists looking for a pleasurable way to learn Spanish.

The highlands are dotted with small villages, some close to metropolitan centers. One of these is the popular Mayan village of San Antonio Aguascalientes, which lies, as does Antigua, in the Quinizalapa valley between the towering volcanoes of Agua (Water) and Fuego (Fire). At times the village is embraced by bright sunshine or shrouded in clouds, much as the lives of the inhabitants are. As has been commented, it is not easy to live between fire and water. (See Sheldon Annis' book, *God and Production in a Guate-*

malan Town.) Despite the hardships that the villagers endure, many have taken advantage of their close proximity to Antigua to market their textiles for modest profits. San Antonio is especially known for its skilled weavers. Many families subsist on the intricate, fine weavings that are produced mostly by the women (see Chapter 3). Although most families have *milpas*, which are small plots of land where they can grow their traditional crops and keep their animals, few of these are large enough for subsistence. Families must find other ways to make ends meet.

Other villages remain quite isolated, with people living fairly dispersed and existing meagerly on their *milpas*, which grow corn, beans and vegetables. The climate in this area depends on altitude and ranges from *tierra templada* (temperate) in the lower areas to *tierra fría* (cold) above 5,446 feet. There is a wet season, called *invierno* (winter) during the months of May to October and a dry one, called *verano* (summer), which lasts from November through April.

The mountains in the western area are the highest, with Mt. Tajamulco rising to 13,800 feet. There are numerous lakes in the highlands; the most spectacular is Lake Atitlán. Ringed by the volcanoes Atitlán, San Pedro and Tolimán, which have various Mayan villages at their bases, the sparkling waters of Lake Atitlán leave a spectator quite dazzled at the beauty of this natural resource.

The peasants are able to augment their farming through fishing, and it is a common sight to see fishermen in wooden kayaks paddling through the waters. A tale that has been passed down through generations describes how abundant native fish inhabited the lake until a foreign entrepreneur stocked it with Japanese black bass to attract more tourists for deep-water fishing. As a result, the black bass ate many of the native fish, and as the bass lie in deeper water, the Mayas are not able to catch them without the expensive equipment that only the tourists have. Although the lake is quite large, it has attracted few foreign fishermen. However, the town of Panajachel on the shores of the lake has become a major tourist attraction. The town has grown rapidly in recent years. Mostly makeshift stalls laden with brightly colored Mayan weavings, jewelry, pottery and other artwork line the streets, and Mayan vendors of all ages peddle their wares. Many young Mayan girls and boys begin their lifelong work by selling products for their families from the neighboring villages of San Antonio Palopó, San Marcos, San Pedro, San Andrés and Santiago Atitlán. Panajachel has also become quite populated with local and foreign artists of the hippie type, and it has become a center for cultural and artistic interchanges.

The other major tourist area that bedazzles the eye is the Mayan village of Chichicastenango, in the heart of the area of Quiché. The name of the town is taken from the plant *chichicaste*, which is a broad-leaf, spiked plant that is quite common in the highlands. *Tenango* means "place of," and various towns in the highlands end with that suffix; hence the town is the place of the *chichicastes*.

Market days are extremely important in the highland areas. Generally held biweekly, they are occasions for people in various villages to come together to trade and obtain necessary products that are not available in their own villages. In Chichicastenango and in other villages, the tourist trade has become quite lucrative. In Chichi, as it is called locally, market days are Thursdays and Sundays. The thousands of Mayas who live in nearby villages flood the town to market their wares. It is an unforgettable experience to awaken at daybreak and walk into the rising mist as the vendors, dressed in their brilliantly colored traditional dress, set up their weavings, which range in color from deep purples, dark red and intense blues to hundreds of other shades. The women's bright *huipiles* (blouses), which identify their place of origin, and their *cortes* (skirts) and *fajas* (sashes) create a kaleidoscope of colors that astounds the eye. In addition, two Catholic churches, Santo Tomás and Calvario, face each other on the main plaza. The steps in front of Santo Tomás are covered by resplendent shades of blooming flowers that Mayan vendors sell. The burning of *copal* (incense) permeates the atmosphere with a sweet aroma and rises in dark streaks toward the early morning sky. Surrounded by the amazing colors and the varied tones of Mayan languages, many newcomers experience the feeling of being in a time and place that is centuries past.

The third geographical area is the Pacific lowlands, a narrow strip about 30 miles wide and about 200 miles long that is bordered on the southwest by Mexico and on the southeast by El Salvador. It is a coastal plane with mostly grasslands that are sprinkled intermittently with forests. Its rich soil, which is fed by volcanic ash, has made it the most productive agricultural center of Guatemala. Coffee plantations are in the higher coastal areas. Sugarcane, cotton plantations and cattle ranches are in the lower coastal plateau. The climate is *tierra caliente* (hot and humid) although there is a dry season during which irrigation is needed for the crops. It is mostly populated by Ladinos, although the Mayan Indians make up the bulk of seasonal workers.

As one can see, Guatemala is a country with a wide spectrum of geographical and climatic variances, and its people have adapted their ways of life to the diverse nuances of their surroundings. Agriculture remains the principal source of sustenance, which underscores the absolute importance of land to

Guatemalans. However, in 1979 it was estimated that 2.2 percent of land-holders owned 65 percent of the land, while 89.7 percent of farmers had access to 16 percent of the land (Cohen and Rosenthal, 1983). Since then, the situation has worsened as more land is consolidated into the hands of large landholders while the peasant population's dependence on agriculture has increased. This is why it is common to see Mayas working their *milpas* on steep, terraced slopes by the highways, miles from their homes, as this is frequently the only land that is available to them. Land continues to be sacred to the Mayas and necessary for their survival. It is a symbol of power and a source of wealth to the non-Indians.

REFERENCES

Annis, Sheldon. *God and Production in a Guatemalan Town.* Austin: University of Texas Press, 1987.

Cohen, Isaac, and Gert Rosenthal. "The Dimensions of Economic Policy Space in Central America." In R. Fagan and O. Pellicer, eds., *The Future of Central America: Policy Choices for the U.S. and Mexico.* Stanford, CA: Stanford University Press, 1983. 15–34.

Falla, Ricardo. *Masacres de la Selva.* Guatemala City: Universidad de San Carlos, 1992. (Also available in translation as *Massacres in the Jungle.* Julia Howland, trans. Foreword and epilogue by Beatriz Manz. Boulder, CO: Westview Press, 1994.)

Fischer, Edward F., and R. Mckenna Brown. *Maya Cultural Activism in Guatemala.* Austin: University of Texas Press, 1996.

Garzon, Susan, R. Mckenna Brown, Julia Becker Richards, and Wuqu'Ajpub'. *The Life of Our Language.* Austin: University of Texas Press, 1998.

Handy, Jim. *Gift of the Devil.* Boston: South End Press, 1984.

Herring, Hubert. *A History of Latin America.* New York: Alfred A. Knopf, 1972.

Hough, R. *Land and Labor in Guatemala: An Assessment.* Guatemala City: Ediciones Papiro, 1983.

Jonas, Susan, and David Tobias, eds. *Guatemala.* Berkeley: North American Congress of Latin America, 1974.

Lovell, George. *Conquest and Survival in Colonial Guatemala.* Montreal: McGill-Queen's University Press, 1992.

Macleod, M. J. *Spanish Central America: A Socioeconomic History, 1520–1720.* Berkeley: University of California Press, 1973.

Monteforte Toledo, Mario. *Centro América: subdesarrollo y dependencia.* Mexico, D.F.: UNAM, 1975.

Nyrop, Richard T., ed. *Guatemala: A Country Study.* Washington, DC: The American University, Foreign Area Studies, 1983.

Paige, J. M. *Agrarian Revolution: Social Movements and Export Agriculture in the Underdeveloped World.* New York: Free Press, 1976.

Smith, Carol. *Guatemalan Indians and the State: 1540 to 1988*. Austin: University of Texas Press, 1990.

Tedlock, Dennis, trans. *Popol Vuh: The Mayan Book of the Dawn of Life*. New York: Simon & Schuster, 1985.

Warren, Kay. *The Symbolism of Subordination*. Austin: University of Texas Press, 1989.

Wolf, Eric R. "Closed Corporate Peasant Communities in Mesoamerica and Central Java." *Southwestern Journal of Anthropology* 13.1 (1957): 1–18.

2

Religion

BEFORE THE ARRIVAL of the Spaniards, the Mayas had their own belief systems that were based on deities associated with the natural world. Mountains, volcanoes and bodies of water were considered earth deities, while the sun, the moon and other heavenly bodies represented supreme beings of the sky. Native priests interpreted natural trauma, in the form of storms, floods, eruptions or earthquakes, as predictions, messages or punishments from the numerous supreme beings. Various rituals and ceremonies took place to please and placate the gods and goddesses. When the Spaniards arrived with their Christian-missionary zeal at the end of the fifteenth century, mass voluntary or coerced conversions took place during which thousands of Mayas apparently accepted the Christian god as the one true supreme god. However, as will be seen in this chapter, many Mayas continued to worship their pre-Columbian deities but disguised their practices by combining them with Christian rituals. This combination of native and European religions is known as syncretism, in which elements of both systems fuse to create something new that has roots in the original belief systems. Today most Guatemalans are Catholics. Yet syncretism is visible, for example, in the images of saints who have Christian names but resemble Mayan deities, and in the practices of the Mayan religious brotherhoods. In recent years, especially since the earthquake of 1976, Evangelical sects have flourished and are transforming religious practices and rituals.

RELIGIOUS BROTHERHOODS

During colonial times in the highlands of Guatemala, two kinds of religious organizations existed, the *guachibal* and the *cofradía*. The *guachibal* was an individual or private practice in which a person kept an image of a certain saint in his or her home; the principal obligation of the individual was to observe the Christian celebrations that were associated with that saint's day. This consisted of a mass, a procession and festivities. The native belief system, with traditional Mayan dances and song, was incorporated into the Christian celebration. The duties associated with caring for the saint were inherited, so that the descendants of the original guardian continued to care for the image of the saint and observe the celebrations associated with it. It appears that at times the original "owner" of the image became associated with the saint, so the celebrations of the saint's day also became a commemoration of the "owner" (Hill, 1986). The Spanish clergy did not interfere much in the *guachibal* as it was an individual or family affair. However, it seems that in certain areas where the image was kept in the church, the Spanish interference was greater. The clergy would charge the "owner" fees to house the saint, threatening to evict the saint if the "owner" did not pay them or if the "owner" could not hold the celebrations on the day of the saint as was customary.

The origins of the *guachibal* are not clear. Some believe that the practice existed among the Mayas before the arrival of the Spaniards, while others believe that it originated with the Spanish clergy, which could pass on the obligations associated with the saint to the indigenous people. The *guachibal* existed as a popular practice up until the eighteenth century, although in certain areas it seems that remnants of it still persist.

Cofradías are religious brotherhoods that are still in existence today. They are composed of a group of followers who venerate and care for a certain saint. The brotherhoods were common in Spain, existing as religious or trade brotherhoods. The Spaniards brought them to the Americas; the Mayas adopted the institution and molded it to fit their own needs under Spanish colonial rule. As opposed to the *guachibal*, the *cofradía* is a group effort to maintain the cult of the saint, and the members are not permanent but are elected and replaceable every year (Hill, 1986).

The indigenous *cofradía* began to function around the second half of the sixteenth century. The Spanish clergy used it as a principal source of income for the church at the local level, as a means to strengthen their control and as a way to propagate the Christian faith. Many of the *cofradías* were associated with religious orders, and the monks and priests took full advantage of the *cofradías* to spread Christian dogma while receiving payment for the various activities associated with the saint. The members of the *cofradías* were responsible for taking care of the images of the saints in the church and for assuming the costs of the celebration for the particular patron saint. They also performed all kinds of tasks for which they were not paid, such as repairing the church. However, the Mayan *cofradía* took on its own syncretic characteristics, evolving in a different manner from the Ladino and Spanish ones. For example, as in the *guachibal,* the ceremonies carry a pre-Columbian, native flavor in the rituals and symbols, in the veneration of ancestors and in the linguistic mixture of Mayan-Spanish languages. In some cases the pre-Columbian element is so predominant that other Christian organizations, such as Acción Católica (Catholic Action) and Evangelical sects, shun them as pagan.

Originally, the *cofradías'* primary function was to assure the spiritual well-being of the brothers. But soon it extended into social services, such as visiting the sick, paying for funerals and the masses to save a member's soul, providing economic aid to widows of members and, during times of economic plenitude, constructing hospitals for ill members and their families (Alejos García, 1982). The costs were paid by dues or by fines collected from those who failed in their duties.

To be a member of a *cofradía* is considered of great importance and esteem in the local community. The members must act according to *costumbre* (tradition), which is based on an egalitarian ideology that stems from Christ and the saints. Members must act with dignity in imitation of their deities, respect their elders and obey the elected officials of the group in their private and social lives. They must participate in all the functions, pay their dues, and work for the betterment of the *cofradía.* This includes buying ornaments, wax, wine and hosts, and carrying out physical tasks that can take them away from their regular jobs. Generally, the egalitarian principle is emphasized in that the *cofradías* make decisions through unanimity, which at times may require numerous meetings to reach consensus. Each year, members are responsible for the expenses incurred during the feast day of the saint. In some cases one member is responsible for the entire year's expenses, bringing him great prestige, responsibility and considerable expense. The expenses include paying for the mass, the candles, the liquor, the food and the marimba band for the festivities of the entire town. For this reason the *cofradías* have been categorized as a "leveling" agent (Nash, 1970), in that by the end of the year the individual has spent all of his savings, sometimes has borrowed heavily, and starts out the next year in poverty. As all members must take on this duty at some point, no one is able to accumulate riches so all remain at the same economic level.

The *cofradías* have been a source of cohesion at the local level. But they have also been a source of conflict as some of them have been rife with financial corruption when associated with fraudulent political figures who use them for their own purposes. The *cofradías* have been criticized for the debauchery of their festivities, in which drunkenness and promiscuity are common. Other religious organizations accuse them of violating the ethics of Christ and their patron saints in the very celebration that is supposed to honor them. Today they are declining in numbers and popularity due to the interference of external agents such as the Acción Católica and political parties. The massive political repression in the 1970s and 1980s and the Evangelical groups who have mushroomed in Guatemala and divided the Mayas are also factors. However, many *cofradías* still function as important symbolic and cohesive brotherhoods, so most likely they will continue to adapt to the changing times and survive well into the new millennium.

However, another form of informal brotherhood exists that, according to some, has a more long-lasting future than the *cofradías* do. This is the system of *compadrazgo*, which functions like the relationship between a family and the godparents of their children. Males associated in this way (for instance, the father and godfather of a child) are called *compadres*; females are called *comadres*. *Compadrazgo* is a tangle of interpersonal relationships based on spiritual relationships that the Catholic Church recognizes. Godparents become *compadres* through baptism, confirmation, matrimony or other spiritual and religious rituals (Castañeda-Medinilla, 1982). *Compadres* and *comadres* take their duties very seriously, and they are available to lend a helping hand, spiritually or materially, in times of duress. Upon the untimely death of the parents, it is the godparents' responsibility to ensure the well-being of the orphaned children. This deep-rooted *compadrazgo* system works for Ladinos and Mayas alike.

CATHOLICISM

Most Guatemalans are Roman Catholic, although their Catholicism may take various forms. For instance, most Mayas have been traditionally Catholic, as evidenced by the long existence of the Catholic *cofradías*. However, to some the *cofradías* are more pagan than Catholic, and they have been accused of confusing the image of their patron saints with the actual saint. But because there was a scarcity of priests in the highlands during the late nineteenth and throughout the twentieth century, lay catechists acted as substitutes for the priests, and the *cofradías* became a way of maintaining reverence for the Catholic Church.

While the Catholic Church had a strong presence throughout the country during the Colonial period and the first half of the nineteenth century, its influence diminished in Guatemala with the strong anticlerical stance of the liberals in the late nineteenth and the first half of the twentieth centuries. Under the presidency of Justo Rufino Barrios (1871–1885), the central role of the Catholic Church was abolished. Properties and goods of the church were confiscated. Special privileges for the clergy were eliminated. Religious schools were nationalized. Foreign clergy were deported. This anti-Catholic leaning continued through the presidency of Jacobo Arbenz Guzmán, which lasted until 1954. It was in 1948 that Archbishop Marino Rossell y Arellano sought to counter anti-Catholic sentiment on a large scale by introducing Acción Católica, an organized group of secular, orthodox Catholics meant to offset the lack of clergy and diminish the influence of the *cofradías* in the highlands (Warren, 1989). The introduction of these lay groups into the Mayan communities, who had their own brand of evangelism and catechists, inevitably led to a clash with the *cofradías* and the Mayan elders. Acción Católica perceived the expensive feasts in honor of the patron saint of the *cofradía* to be ritual waste. It believed that the drunkenness and adultery common at the feasts were contrary to Catholic dogma. The long-serving members of the *cofradías* considered Acción Católica to be out of touch with the customs and rituals of their people. These tensions continue today, although with the advent of Evangelical sects the influence of the *cofradías* has diminished considerably.

With the overthrow of Arbenz Guzmán in 1954 and the imposition of military dictators until 1986, the position of the Catholic Church in Guatemala has strengthened. Seen as a barrier to communism, the right-wing military dictators granted the Catholic Church more powers, allowing religious instruction in schools and permitting the increase of clergy and dioceses throughout Guatemala. However, in the 1970s and 1980s the number of priests in Guatemala was quite limited in comparison to other Latin American countries, and the vast majority of them were foreigners. Foreign missionaries also flocked to the highlands, contributing to the existing divisions brought about by the tensions between Acción Católica and the *cofradías*. Foreign Catholic priests and missionaries had resources that they could depend on from parishes in their own countries, which made them able to act independently of contributions from the Guatemalan upper class. They began multiple projects to improve conditions in the Mayan communities, such as farming and textile cooperatives, literacy campaigns and children's education. These projects were viewed with growing suspicion and dismay by the government, the upper classes and the traditional hierarchy of the Catholic Church, who were all caught up in the fervent anticommunist waves that swept the country in the 1970s and 1980s. Organizing cooperatives and educating Indians were seen as dangerous activities, inspired by foreign communist sympathizers. As the war against the guerrillas intensified and the violence spread throughout the highlands, many priests, missionaries and lay workers spoke out against the repression that they witnessed in their communities. Some were influenced by liberation theology and attempted to intervene when the army arrived to punish the "subversives," those Mayan men, women and children who happened to live in villages that the guerrillas occasionally visited to collect supplies. This increased the suspicion that the Catholics were all radical leftists in league with the guerrillas. As a result, Catholicism became associated with communism, and many Catholic priests, nuns and catechists were murdered in the Guatemalan highlands during the 1970s and 1980s; Others were deported. The aftershocks of the violence still shake the highland communities at the end of the second millennium. To be Catholic continues to have political implications in the highland communities.

PROTESTANTISM

Although Protestants arrived in Guatemala at the end of the nineteenth century, brought in as part of President Rufino Barrios' anti-Catholic program, their numbers were not significant until the 1940s and 1950s. They were initially appealing to mostly lower-income Ladinos looking for ways to better their lot. As the Protestant message focuses on individual improvement through hard work, sobriety and chastity, it was seen as a welcome alternative to traditional Catholicism and its message of self-sacrifice and self-effacement for the good of the church and the community. For these same reasons Protestantism began to appeal to the indigenous people, and many Mayas broke with their *cofradías* or orthodox Catholic groups to convert to Protestantism. Fundamentalist sects that were even more focused on the individual began to grow in number and gradually became more influential than the conventional Protestants were. In part, this may be attributed to political and economic reasons. When Efraín Ríos Montt, an Evangelical, became president in 1982 and continued to implement the military repression in the highlands, many Mayas converted to protect themselves from the Catholic-communist stigma that the soldiers frequently targeted. And as all Evangelical congregations were connected to parishes in the United States, they were able to offer resources that were extremely attractive to the impoverished: food, clothing, medicines, and so on. In times of distress, which were and are frequent among most Mayas, these benefits work as a powerful incentive. After the earthquake of 1976, Evangelical preachers were quick to thunder that it was a sign of God's wrath on the slothful ways of the nonconverted. Many believed them, and Evangelical congregations mushroomed throughout Guatemala (Annis, 1987).

By some estimates about one-third of Guatemalans currently belong to fundamentalist sects (Garrard-Burnett, 1998). In the highlands this has deepened the religious divisions, especially since the Evangelical position on drinking and celibacy is contrary to the practices of the *cofradías*. However, the popularity of the Evangelicals is attributed in some measure to exactly that stance. As alcoholism is a rampant problem among the Indians, Mayan women are especially attracted to a religion in which, theoretically, their husbands will stay sober and faithful.

Mayan opponents to the Evangelical sects object that their basic precept, focusing on the person's relationship to God and individual self-improvement, erodes the traditional sense of community, respect for the ancestors and cultural identity among the Maya. Evangelical preachers, for example, exhort their followers to improve themselves economically by modernizing, which frequently means abandoning Mayan rituals and traditions that they perceive as wasteful. Mayan women are encouraged to stop wearing *traje* (Mayan dress) and to take advantage of the tourist trade to sell their *huipiles* instead. Foreign anthropologists have jumped into the fray and argue passionately on either side of the debate. Some believe that the Mayas' only chance to escape their poverty-stricken, subordinate position and become an important force in Guatemala is to leave their old ways behind and join the modern world. Others insist that the old ways are not an impediment to an economically modern society, but rather they are what lend the Mayas their strength, perseverance and unique cultural identity. The Mayan revitalization movement certainly demonstrates that Mayas are capable of being Maya and modern at the same time.

Whatever the outcome, today it is common to walk into a village in highland Guatemala and see Evangelical sects, Acción Católica and *cofradías*. All are in competition with each other. In fact, during prayer, certain formerly quiet towns become quite noisy. Rival houses of worship, sometimes next door to each other, sing as loudly as possible to drown the other out.

REFERENCES

Alejos García, José. "Naturaleza y Perspectiva de la Cofradía Indígena en Guatemala." *Guatemala Indígena* 17.1–2 (1982): 89–158.

Annis, Sheldon. *God and Production in a Guatemalan Town.* Austin: University of Texas Press, 1987.

Castañeda-Medinilla, José. "¿Cofradía o gobierno tribal?" *Guatemala Indígena* 17.1–2 (1982): 89–95.

Foster, George. "Cofradía y Compadrazgo en España é Hispano-América." *Guatemala Indígena* 1.1 (1961): 107–47.

Garrard-Burnett, Virginia. *Protestantism in Guatemala: Living in the New Jerusalem.* Austin: University of Texas Press, 1998.

Hill, Robert M., II. "Manteniendo el culto a los santos: aspectos financieros de las instituciones religiosas en el altiplano colonial maya." *Mesoamérica* 7.11 (1986): 61–77.

Nash, June. *In the Eyes of the Ancestors: Belief and Behavior in a Maya Community.* New Haven: Yale University Press, 1970.

Nyrop, Richard T., ed. *Guatemala: A Country Study.* Washington, DC: The American University, Foreign Area Studies, 1983.

Saler, Benson. "Religious Conversion and Self-Aggrandizement: A Guatemalan Case." *Practical Anthropology* 12.3 (May–June 1965): 107–14.

Smith, Carol. *Guatemalan Indians and the State: 1540 to 1988.* Austin: University of Texas Press, 1990.

Tortolani, Paul. "Political Participation of Native and Foreign Catholic Clergy in Guatemala." *Journal of Church and State* 15.3 (1973): 407–18.

Warren, Kay. *The Symbolism of Subordination.* Austin: University of Texas Press, 1989.

3

Social Customs

MANY SOCIAL CUSTOMS in Guatemala are practiced by Ladinos and Mayas alike. Catholic religious celebrations and rituals, such as Christmas and Holy Week, are common to most Guatemalans. The numerous fairs generally associated with the celebration of the patron saint of a city or village, such as the Fair of Jocotenango, are also held in common. The more pagan-tinged All Saints' Day is also ritualized throughout Guatemala, although it has different and creative forms. Various beliefs combine Mayan and Christian elements, reflecting a folklore that has been handed down through generations. Maximón, the irreverent, cigar-smoking saint of the Mayan village of Santiago Atitlán, is popular among Mayas and Ladinos alike. Many oral histories, myths and legends have their roots in a pre-Columbian past but have been modified to fit into a Christian, Ladino version. Other beliefs are not shared by both groups. In the highlands, for instance, many Mayas believe that animal spirits, known as *nahuales*, inhabit the human spirit. This belief is not generally shared by Ladinos.

An important social custom, weaving, is integral to the Mayan way of life. It reflects their ancestral customs and traditions, and it affects their economic well-being in the modern world. Weaving and *traje* are viewed as major cultural markers among the Mayas. Cuisine is another marker. Although some foods are common to all Guatemalans, the different dishes prepared and consumed are determined, to a large degree, by their geographic location, which is tied to a group's ethnic identity. Garífuna cuisine, for example, reflects the tropical nature of its surroundings. It is made up of recipes handed down through generations of African ancestors.

Festivals constitute an important element in the social life of a community. They serve as an instrument of social cohesion and as a way of affirming one's traditional values and customs. In Guatemala they serve to reveal the social order that predominates in the different communities, reflecting communal roles and habits. They are an important source of information, as most of the economic and social activities of a community are integrated into the festival. They are also an outlet for the popular arts and folklore.

Christmas Festivities

In Guatemala a long cycle of festivals associated with Christmas begins at the end of October, when children and young adults start their vacations from school that last until the beginning of January (much like the three months of summer vacation in the United States). This is a festive time for the young well-to-do, who find themselves with free time to dedicate to antics such as kite flying (kites are called *barriletes* or *cometas*). Depending on the particular historic, political and economic moment, it is a time of anticipation throughout the population for the coming Christmas holiday.

One popular feast is La Quema del Diablo (Devil's Day), which seems to have originated from the fires lit during colonial times for the procession of the Immaculate Conception, which is on the evening of December 7. Fires (*luminarias* or *fogatas*) were lit along the streets so that those participating in the procession could see their way. It came to symbolize the defeat of the devil by the Immaculate Conception. The feast became widely popular. Today thousands of streets in Guatemala are lit by these fires, which fill the streets with luminous lights and smoke. Firecrackers are wildly popular in Guatemala, and this feast is accompanied by an abundance of them, set off to celebrate the triumph of the Virgin Mary over the devil (Luján Muñoz, 1981). As the Franciscans especially revere the Immaculate Conception, in areas of Franciscan domain stalls are set up to sell fritters, fried bananas, *atol* (corn- or rice-based drinks), coffee and chocolate.

The actual celebration of the Immaculate Conception, which falls on December 8, derives from a long tradition originating in Spain and popular throughout Latin America. In the first capital of Guatemala in its second location it is an extremely important feast because the town was named Concepción Ciudad Vieja after the Immaculate Conception. It is celebrated with traditional dances, such as the Dance of the Moors and Christians, the usual fireworks, and *loas*, short theatrical pieces originally intended to be part of the intermission for full-length plays. These popular pieces generally feature a personified Virgin of the Conception defeating the devil, who flees in humiliation. A similar kind of celebration takes place in Guatemala City on December 12 for the feast of the Virgin of Guadalupe.

December 16 marks the beginning of the festivities for the *novena*, a nine-day ritual that culminates with the birthday of Christ on December 25. Called *las posadas* in Mexico and Guatemala, the populace symbolically accompanies the Virgin Mary and Joseph in their travails as they unsuccessfully search for *posada* (shelter) until December 24. In Guatemala City groups of children dressed as pilgrims carry candles and lanterns and walk through the streets singing until they reach a specific house, where they plead for shelter. A playful banter ensues, with those inside refusing to give them shelter until they realize that the pilgrims represent Mary and Joseph. Then they let the group in to prayer and merriment, accompanied by food and drink.

Christmas dinner for family and friends is usually shared on Christmas Eve before midnight. Generally, it consists of the traditional black or red tamales, turkey, sweetbreads and chocolate, with liquor to toast the birth of Christ at midnight. Shortly before midnight on December 24, an immense amount of fireworks, ranging from the grandiose to the humble, are set off. Even impoverished families manage to accumulate firecrackers to participate in the occasion. This is when some children receive their gifts, supposedly brought by the Niño Dios, the Christ child. Midnight mass is also celebrated (called the *Misa del Gallo*), although it has become less common in recent years.

On December 25, children who did not open their presents the night before do so. The day is full of activities. Children play with their new presents and each other. Family and friends gather around the *nacimiento* (manger). Most people attend mass at noon, at which time another round of firecrackers is set off.

The *nacimiento* is an altar set up to commemorate the birth of Jesus Christ, much like the manger scenes in the United States. However, in Guatemala the varied interpretations of the scene reflect the cultural and ethnic blend of its population. The central figures are always Mary, Joseph and the baby Jesus. They are generally accompanied by shepherds, animals and the *reyes magos* (three kings of Orient). Then the possibilities are endless. Some people create elaborate backgrounds that represent their own natural surroundings, with mountains, valleys, rivers, waterfalls and other flora or fauna of the region. The human landscape consists of figures made of multicolored wood, wax or clay, dressed in cotton or wool clothing, representing Mayas, Ladinos and figures associated with everyday life, such as the washerwoman, corn grinder, musician, vendor and bus driver and mythological creatures. This turns the *nacimiento* into a true representation of Guatemalan folklore (Luján Muñoz, 1981).

The various themes associated with the Christmas festivities, such as the Annunciation, the Visitation, the Birth of Christ, the Adoration of the Shepherds and the Three Kings of Orient, are rich with iconographic possibilities that have been explored in drawings, paintings, sculptures, engravings and prints. They range from formal, polished representations to informal, popular depictions by indigenous and nonindigenous artists. Popular theater also promotes these themes in the form of *loas* (short theatrical pieces), which are dedicated to the Immaculate Conception or the Virgin of Guadalupe, and in *pastorelas* (lyrical pieces), which are recited by shepherds revering the infant Jesus. Lyrical poetry in the form of *villancicos* (interludes of song and dance) are composed for the occasion. They are sung to simple tunes in processions or in church. In some *villancicos* the language can be a blend of Mayan terms or African words mixed with a particular variety of Spanish (Luján Muñoz, 1981). (The famous *villancicos* of the seventeenth century Mexican nun, Sor Juana Inés de la Cruz, is a good example of this ethnic linguistic blend.)

On December 28, Guatemalans celebrate the Día de los Inocentes (Day of the Innocents), in which children and some adults play pranks on each other, akin to April Fool's Day in the United States. New Year's Eve is a social event that has the usual deafening profusion of fireworks right before midnight, which is repeated to a lesser degree the next day at noon. On January 1, mass is obligatory for Catholics. January 6, the Día de los Reyes (Day of the Kings), was traditionally when children received their gifts according to Spanish custom. It no longer has much importance as the children receive their gifts on Christmas Eve or Christmas Day. But the belief in *cabañuelas*, also a Spanish tradition, still exists. Accordingly, the first twelve days of the year are considered omens for the corresponding months. So if there is bad weather on the third day, the third month will bring bad weather. On January 25, the *novena* dedicated to the Christ child begins. This ends on February 2, the day of the Virgin of Candelaria, which is celebrated with prayer, song, the inevitable fireworks and a dinner of tamales, chocolate and sweetbreads. The next day the *nacimiento* is taken down and packed away for the following year. This date corresponds to forty days after Christmas.

There are numerous variations to the cycle of Christmas festivities described above. In some indigenous communities, for example, the *cofradías* generally play an important part in the rituals. Dances are performed, and large ceremonial dinners are accompanied by musicians playing *tambores* (drums) and *pitos* (whistles). Recitals are in the Mayan languages. On Christmas Eve the images of the Virgin Mary and Joseph are taken in procession to the church to hear midnight mass.

All Saints' Day and All Souls' Day

All Saints' Day on November 1, and All Souls' Day on November 2, are observed throughout Latin America with a variety of rituals that reflect cultural beliefs and patterns associated with the dead. For some people the dead have simply passed on to another dimension from which they may return periodically. In Guatemala, as well as elsewhere, it is believed that on November 1, to commemorate the saints, and November 2, to remember those souls in purgatory, the dead are released from the underworld and are free to wander among the living. If the living family and friends do not welcome them with offerings of their favorite food and drink, then the dead may punish them with illness, crop failure or other disasters. Therefore, the families decorate their houses and set an offering of liquor, bread, fruit, *atol*, candles and/or the dead's favorite food for s/he to consume during this period. The families and friends also visit and decorate the tomb, spending the day in the cemetery among groups of other people. They leave candles and food by the tomb.

All Saints' Day and All Souls' Day have taken on a special, colorful flavor in the Mayan village of Santiago Sacatepéquez. The village has become renowned for its enormous, spectacular kites that are flown in the cemeteries during these two days. The kites, ranging from ten to twenty feet, are flown by four to six young men who keep the kite in the air for an hour or two. The sky becomes festooned with dozens of these brilliantly colored kites. Even the cemetery below becomes colorful when the kites inevitably crash.

What is the connection between kite flying and the Days of the Dead? Boys flying small kites are common throughout the highlands, especially in the windy month of November. Cemeteries, which are generally flat and devoid of trees, are an ideal place to fly kites. They became part of the entertainment for the families visiting the dead in the cemeteries on November 1 and 2. In Santiago three young men built a huge kite in 1940 that attracted great attention. After that, other young men joined in to create even bigger and better kites. Almost all young men in Santiago belong to a group of four to eight members who begin working on the kite many weeks prior to the event. They build the kite in the evenings after working in the field all day. They discuss each step of the kite-making process. Decisions are made by consensus. The kites are built with hundreds of sheets of colored tissue paper, bamboo poles, rope and old clothes for the twenty-foot tail (Smith, 1978).

Although some believe that the kites are messengers that communicate with the dead, anthropologist Kenneth W. Smith, who spent time studying the event in Santiago, believes that the practice became a way of attracting single, young women of the town, who were generally inaccessible during most of the year, as virtuous women should not be seen conversing openly or flirting with men. Flaunting their workmanship and physical prowess by flying the huge kites, the young men attracted attention to themselves and, hopefully, gained the admiration of the desired young woman, opening the door for possible courtship.

During the night of November 1 another ritual is practiced. A large group of young Mayan men follow leaders of the *cofradía* Saint Michael the Archangel through town, banging on doors and yelling for pots. When a door is opened, they charge into the house, howling for pots until they find broken ones that have been purposely set aside for them. They take the pots outside and smash them on the streets. In this way they startle the spirits of the dead who are still lurking among the living, and send them back to the underworld.

The Fair of Jocotenango

The Feria de Jocotenango (Fair of Jocotenango) is the most important festival in Guatemala City. It is celebrated in August to honor the Virgin Mary of the Assumption, the patron saint of the city. Today the fair takes place in the northern sector of Guatemala City, which is where the neighborhood of Jocotenango used to be until it was swallowed up by the ever-expanding city. The fair originated, however, in the town of Jocotenango on the outskirts of the old capital, which is now Antigua. Jocotenango, meaning "place of abundant fruit," was an indigenous village that inaugurated the festival in 1620 upon construction of their church, which was dedicated to the Virgin Mary of the Assumption (Pardo, Zamora and Luján, 1969). At that time it was a feast that the *guachibales* sponsored. It consisted of an important fair and traditional dances, lasting from August 14 to 31 of each year.

Mayas from all over Guatemala, Ladinos and important government officials attended the fair, which exhibited brilliantly colored weavings, spices, fruits, chocolate and other products. But in 1773 an earthquake destroyed the old capital. The new capital was established in 1776, where it stands today. In Jocotenango, where the church, the public fountains and the water tank were intact, the Indians resisted moving despite orders from government officials. The local priest even removed the images of the revered saints from the church and transported them to the new Jocotenango, but the Mayas were still reluctant to leave their ancestral lands to become part of a body of forced labor. They were finally forcibly evacuated to makeshift and inadequate shelters on the edge of the city, where they served as an unpaid labor force to build the new city. There the men labored as bricklayers, construction workers and beasts of burden, while the women served as wet nurses for the wealthy Ladinas.

It is believed that the first fair celebrated in the new Jocotenango was in August of 1804. It gradually assumed the same popularity that it had in the old Jocotenango, with products arriving from all over Guatemala to be exhibited in disorderly profusion. A report in 1906 described the products that vendors sold at the fair. The goods from various villages in the western highlands included apples, nuts, bread from San Diego, clay whistles from Patzún, guitars from Totonicapán, ponchos and woolen cloths from Momostenango, vases, rosaries and sweets (Meléndez, 1983). In the twentieth century the fair took on different aspects, depending on who assumed the presidency. During one period it became a place for the rich to exhibit their elegant clothing and carriages. During another period it was a center for horse racing, gambling, cattle exhibitions and artisanal products, such as weaving, ceramics and other forms of pottery.

Today the Fair of Jocotenango takes place from August 13 to 15. It is a popular and traditional affair, a major market that sells all kinds of products and still attracts Mayas, Ladinos and numerous international tourists.

Holy Week in Antigua

Antigua is famous for its Catholic celebration of Holy Week, which commemorates the Passion, Crucifixion and Resurrection of Jesus Christ. The entire city participates in the event, and thousands of national and international visitors flock to Antigua to witness the dramatic happenings. Taking place sometime between March 22 and April 23, the entire week is full of solemn activities that replicate the Passion and Crucifixion of Christ, culminating in jubilation on Easter. The special flavor of this event arrived with Spanish missionaries from Seville, who brought Andalucian flavor to the religious phenomenon during colonial times (Quintanilla Mesa, 1989).

The event begins on Palm Sunday, during which the venerated images of Jesús Nazareno (Jesus Nazarene) and the Santisima Virgen de Dolores (Holy Virgin of Sorrow) are carried from their churches through the city on the shoulders of devoted followers who carry lanterns while dressed in purple robes with white waistbands. Similar processions that venerate images from various churches occur on Holy Monday, Tuesday, Wednesday and Thursday, replicating the final days of Christ on the earth. On Good Friday the streets of Antigua are carpeted with natural, aromatic rugs of flowers, pines, clover and fruits, which the residents put together and place in front of their homes. There are all kinds and shapes. Some are very long, even up to a kilometer, with colonial, Mayan, Roman or other original designs. At 3:00 A.M., preparations are already underway for the mock trial and sentencing of Christ. Participants dress as Roman soldiers, Pontius Pilate and other participants in the drama. At 7:00 A.M., the revered image of Christ carrying his crucifix is moved through the carpeted main streets of Antigua on the shoulders of his worshipers until early afternoon, when the image is replaced by another of Christ being laid to rest. At 4:30 P.M., Antigua becomes adorned with black crepe paper as thousands of people, burning incense and dressed in black, crowd the plazas and streets. A spectacular procession is led by the man bearing the crucifix, with hundreds of followers carrying black banners and standards engraved with the final words of Christ and the pronouncements of God. Life-like images representing the archangels, the stations of the cross, Cavalry, the apostles and many others are part of the silent procession through the streets, where multitudes pray quietly. The image of Christ is laid to rest in a church at 11:00 P.M.

Holy Saturday continues with other funeral processions led by the image of a sorrowful Virgen de la Soledad (Virgin of Solitude), followed by numerous women dressed in black who commemorate her moments of sorrow at the side of Christ. Easter Sunday is a time of rejoicing, with early processions through the streets of a festive Antigua celebrating the Resurrection of Christ. Firecrackers are heard throughout the city, and masses are held in all the churches. The week-long ceremonies end that day, and residents return to their daily lives.

THE IMPORTANCE OF WEAVING AND *TRAJE* (DRESS) AS A MARKER OF MAYAN CULTURAL IDENTITY

Wherever one travels in the world today, it is not uncommon to come into contact with two distinct Latin American cultural markers. The icon of the Argentine guerrilla hero, Che Guevara, is represented in hundreds of different ways, such as imprinted images on T-shirts, banners, scarves, wall hangings, portraits, figurines, matchboxes, pencil cases and key chains. The other popular, visually stimulating cultural marker is Guatemalan textiles, which today are distributed worldwide. The brilliant colors of Mayan weavings are represented in traditional Mayan clothing, such as *huipiles* (woven Mayan blouses), Western clothing enhanced with Mayan designs, wall hangings, ribbons, belts, rugs, bedcovers, blankets, purses, backpacks, pot holders, eyeglass cases and so on. In a sense, these two cultural markers are at odds with each other. The first, Che Guevara, represents the struggle of the masses against capitalism, while the other, Mayan textiles, represents the successful incorporation of Mayan traditional crafts into the world marketplace.

Mayan Women's Dress

Mayan women have been weaving for centuries. When the Spaniards arrived, they were astounded by the brightly colored dress of the Mayas. Mayan women traditionally wear *traje*, which is a combination of a skillfully woven, multicolored blouse called a *huipil* and of a *corte*, a woven wraparound skirt that reaches to the ankles, and is held together by a *faja* (sash) at the waist. Women also wear some form of headdress, such as a *pañuelo*, on their heads, or *cintas*, four- or five-foot-long colorful ribbons that are braided into their shiny, long, black hair. A lengthy rectangular *rebozo* (shawl) and a decorated *delantal* (apron) are also part of *traje*. There are also small, silver or gold, round hoops for earrings and, in some areas, necklaces made from glass beads.

The *huipil* is a distinct work of art, woven or embroidered, that may take months to complete. It is distinguished by its design, style, pattern and concept. It varies according to region and individual creativity or taste. The *corte*, which is woven on a treadle or footloom, is composed of about five yards of material that is wrapped several times around a woman's lower body. Although there are certain colors and designs that are traditionally associated with a particular Mayan village, each *huipil* is woven individually on a backstrap loom. No two *huipiles* are identical. The *cortes*, however, generally are not distinctive. When the conquistadors arrived, men also wore colorfully woven apparel, but this is true only in certain areas today.

Traditionally, one could guess the village of origin by the colors and design of the *huipil* that a Mayan woman wore. For instance, a bright *huipil* of predominantly orange and red, interwoven with various minor colors such as green and blue, with a specific geometric pattern, identifies the wearer as a woman from San Antonio Aguascalientes. It has been theorized that the conquistadors imposed a color code on the Mayans upon arrival to more easily account for and control the indigenous population. But this theory has been largely dismissed by contemporary Mayan intellectuals, who demonstrate ample proof through pre-Columbian representations that this was a tradition in place long before the conquistadors ever set foot in the Americas (Otzoy, 1996).

The Looms

Historically, Mayan women (and a few men) grow up weaving on backstrap looms. These are warp yarns stretched between two sticks or end bars that are attached by a backstrap around the hips of the woman at one end, while the other end is affixed by a rope to a tree, bush, post or any similar object. Sticks made from bamboo or pine have various functions, such as controlling the warp and separating the odd from the even-numbered warps (Sperlich and Sperlich, 1980). The backstrap loom can be rolled into a small bundle when not in use, and it is quite portable. Women sit and weave while waiting for a bus, selling their wares at the market, or during spare moments between chores at home.

In contrast to the backstrap loom, the treadle or footloom is a large, unwieldy, wooden contraption that stays in one location. Some Mayan men use the footloom to weave volumes of materials with Mayan colors and patterns, which can then be modified and sold to tourists as tablecloths, napkins, bedspreads, wall hangings, shirts for men, dresses for women, ribbons or numerous other items. Some of these are also woven on backstrap looms. The footloom, however, is more capable of handling large volumes of material that can be used to create articles for tourists, and it takes the place of the backstrap loom in some cases as a more efficient device for producing weavings quickly.

Weaving a *Huipil*

As many Mayan homes do not have electricity, women take advantage of any daylight hours that are not occupied with their numerous other duties to weave. For example, a typical young Mayan woman rises promptly at 5:00 A.M., sweeps the dirt floors with a whisk broom, goes out to see if the chickens have laid any eggs, returns to stoke up the fire in the wood-burning stove, and for the next hour either takes the corn to the miller for grinding or, if they do not have the pennies to pay the miller, helps her mother grind the corn to make the paste for the tortillas. She then pats and shapes dozens of corn tortillas to be cooked over the *comal* (clay platter). This is the fundamental nourishment for the men preparing to go out into the fields. She repeats this task, the *tortillando* (making tortillas), twice more. At noon she walks miles to bring the warm tortillas, beans and rice to the men in the fields. When the men return in the evening, with luck the tortillas are accompanied by *pepián*, a tasty chicken gruel. In between these meals she carries water home for cleaning and drinking purposes. She washes the kitchen utensils, watches over her younger siblings, scrubs clothes either down at the river or at the nearby *pila* (stone washbasins with running water that are set up in neighborhoods for laundry), lays the clothes on the ground or hangs them to dry, sews, goes to the market to sell wares, trade or buy necessary items, and does countless other tasks. This does not leave much time for uninterrupted weaving. The complex patterns of a *huipil* can take several months to finish. A skillful weaver makes a "blueprint" before she begins such a complex project. She chooses her colors, measurements, design and motif carefully for the *huipil*, which is the "most symbolically dense article" of clothing (Hendrickson, 1986). They are generally composed of two rectangular panels woven separately and then sewn together, with a square or round opening at the top for the head and armholes in the sides.

Women start weaving at a very young age, and they gain skill and dexterity with maturity. A girl as young as five may begin weaving a *servilleta* (napkin) that is used to wrap tortillas to keep them warm or cover food or baskets. This begins her apprenticeship, which lasts for several years. Because Mayan weavings have become so popular in the international market, selling the weavings has become an important source of income for a family. Many women will set aside two or three *huipiles*, similar to a savings account, to sell in times of hardship or stress. Also, because selling or trading their weavings has become part of the tourist industry, Mayan women leave the home and travel much more than they did before. Some women do not weave and instead become vendors of Mayan weavings and crafts, traveling to the most popular tourist markets such as Panajachel, Antigua and Chichicastenango. If offered the right price, a woman might sell the *huipil* that she is wearing. For this reason it is no longer easy to identify a woman's village of origin solely by her *huipil*, as she may have replaced the traditional one with one that she bought at a bargain in another village. In fact, some women, especially those belonging to Evangelical sects, give up wearing *huipiles* entirely. They find it more economically lucrative to sell the *huipiles* they weave to tourists and to substitute a cheap, cotton, manufactured blouse to wear along with their *corte*. Other weavers are influenced by designs or motifs that they observe in different villages or among international tourists, which may appear as a variation of the traditional regional design. For instance, one may find *huipiles* with embroidered or woven poodles or rockets, which are not exactly part of the traditional Mayan construction. Or a woman may be struck with an original idea and add a stylistic innovation to a textile that other weavers might widely admire and imitate.

MAYAN WOMEN AND EDUCATION

Many young Mayan women are discovering the value of education. An increasing number of mothers are insisting that not only their sons learn how to read and write, but that their daughters do, too. Because they are still expected to perform the normal daily chores that limit their time, a growing number of young Mayan girls are faced with the choice of attending school or weaving. Weaving a *huipil* is a tremendously time-consuming task, and it does not fetch the same price in Guatemala that it might in another country. In some cases the weaver earns less than a dollar per day. This means that a full-time, forty-hour work week will bring in an income of about five dollars, or thirty dollars for a month's work. Education is increasingly seen as a viable alternative to bettering one's economic and social position in Guatemala. Ironically then, weaving as a means to a better future may gradually be replaced by education, as Mayan women sell their textiles to educate their daughters so that they may find better jobs in which they will not have the time to weave. Thus a usable art may be replaced by a usable vocation in future generations. However, perhaps when education becomes more easily accessible to the Mayas, they can turn that education to preserve the customs and traditions of the past as well as to pave the path to a better future. Efforts by Mayan intellectuals have already borne results in that area, and in recent years far more young Mayas are attending school than those of their parents' generation did. This is having a deep impact on the ways in which Mayas view themselves and their society.

The Importance of *Traje*

Traje, or traditional clothing, has deep cultural significance for the Mayas. It represents a tie to the past and to their ancestors. For historic, political and economic reasons, it is mostly women who are the bearers of this tradition. The daily lives of Mayan women of Guatemala represent the continuance of the customs and traditions of the ancestors. They also represent new survival strategies as they face challenges brought on by shifting political, economic, social and natural factors. One may say that they adopt from their ancestors what is necessary for survival while looking for alternative ways to adapt to changing circumstances. Their lives vary greatly, depending on their particular socioeconomic or political status, the regions in which they live, the time period, their religion, the personal decisions that they make and other factors. However, speaking in general terms, Mayan women's everyday lives are a struggle for survival against poverty, hunger, discrimination and violence from within and without. They are on their feet daily from dawn to dusk, tending to a multitude of domestic tasks. However, they also keep their eyes on the future. At times, however, their traditional ways come into conflict with modern Ladino society, and Mayas are obliged to make difficult choices.

One example is the story of Amanda, a young Mayan woman who grew up in the traditional manner in the highland village of San Martín Jilotepeque. Her mother worked for years as a maid in a convent for pennies a week to support her family and allow her two daughters to attend the Escuela del Socorro, a Catholic school run by nuns in Antigua. This young Mayan woman graduated from high school with honors. She then received a scholarship to attend college in the highland city of Quetzaltenango, where after years of hard work, she acquired a degree in social work. To support herself it was necessary to find employment while studying, and she attempted many times without success to obtain a teaching position in the local schools. Finally, her landlady, a Ladina, advised her to replace her traditional *huipil* and *corte* with Western clothing so that her Mayan identity would not be apparent. Although at first resistant to the idea, her economically desperate situation obliged her to compromise, and she finally went to an interview without her *traje*. She was hired. She said that she will always wonder what would have happened if she had gone to the interview in her *huipil* and *corte*. She also described how she later attended social functions, generally after school, in *traje* and that there did not seem to be any major objections. That is because, she said, "*ya me conocen*" ("they already know me") (Interview with Shea, 1989). In other words, because the Ladinos knew this Mayan woman first as a "person," when she "donned" her Indian identity, she was not immediately stereotyped as inferior. Although she was uncomfortable wearing Western clothing to teach her daily classes, she felt that she was making an impact from within. She had to do away with the most obvious external marker of her ethnicity to gain entrance to the institution that was barring her access. Once inside, she worked to dismantle the stereotypes associated with her culture, hoping that at some point she would be allowed to wear *traje* to teach and that another young Mayan woman who might apply to that school would not be rejected immediately because of her Indian identity. This is only one example of the ways in which educated young Mayas are working both to gain passage into public institutions and to pave the way for future generations of teachers, social workers, professors, doctors, lawyers, administrators, government officials and so on.

Mayan men still wear their traditional dress in certain areas. This consists of cotton shirts that are sometimes designed with elaborate patterns and loose pants. In some areas such as Sololá, wool skirts, hats, woven belts, ponchos and sandals are common. However, a majority of Mayan men now wear Western clothing. This is largely due to economic and political reasons.

As noted, because clothing is the most obvious external ethnic marker in Guatemala, it became the object of discrimination and scorn by the Ladinos. Mayan men historically were the ones who traveled to the city to sell their wares, take care of other business or participate in public life. But the government passed edicts in the nineteenth century, for instance, that prohibited men who wore Mayan clothing from holding public office. So if a Maya wanted to run for a parish office, he would be forced to abandon his native dress and adopt Western clothing (Otzoy, 1996). Also, because discrimination against the Mayas by the Ladinos in the urban centers was as common then as it is today, there were certain advantages to appearing less Maya. By learning Spanish and adopting certain Western cultural patterns, such as using their hard-earned pesos to eat hamburgers and drink Coca-Cola in fast-food restaurants, some Mayas were able to pass as non-Indian, much as some light-skinned African Americans did in the United States. They therefore had a better chance of achieving their goals, or at least of escaping the contempt of the Ladinos.

Both the local and the national bureaucracy were rife with corruption, and Mayas who could not read Spanish were tricked and cheated out of their land and other goods by marking documents that they were told would ensure their claims. Mayas came to understand that they had to learn to speak, read and write Spanish to protect themselves from their oppressors. In this context, speaking and dressing like the Ladinos became advantageous.

The reverence and respect that Mayas accord to their ancestors may be contrasted to the Ladino reaction to the Mayan past and present. Ironically, the Ladinos—speaking in general terms, certainly all are not included— perceive the greatest value of the Mayan culture to be in the ruins left of their city-states, pyramids, temples, ball courts and monuments to a past history. However, they are blind to the Mayan culture that surrounds them, which is the continuance of that history. In addition, they admire Mayan weavings and crafts, but they do not appreciate those who have created the crafts nor those who wear them, such as the Mayan women in their traditional woven *traje*. An example is the Miss Guatemala pageant in which contenders frequently dress up in *traje*, although none of the contestants are Mayan. By relegating the greatness of the Mayas to the past or by praising the crafts while denigrating the living creators of those crafts, many Ladinos are unaware of the human dimensions of those to whom they live in close proximity.

Traje and the "Revitalization" Movement

During the years of violence in the 1970s and 1980s, when tens of thousands of Mayas were murdered indiscriminately and displaced as some 626 Mayan villages were razed, the Mayas clearly experienced the fury that was designed to annihilate their ethnic ways of life. This contributed to an erosion of Mayan cultural identity. However, a small but effective group of young, educated Mayas have led a cultural "revitalization" movement that is designed to renew pride and to honor the value of their cultural heritage. Although many of the men in this movement do not wear the traditional Mayan clothing, some wear specially designed jackets with Mayan patterns, medallions with their Mayan names or signs engraved, Mayan scarves and other articles of clothing that are a blend of Mayan colors and designs with Western styles. In contrast, Mayan women intellectuals continue to wear *traje*.

It is interesting to note certain shifts in Mayan customs and traditions because of the many social and political changes that affect their communities. One of these changes is an alteration in gender roles as women become more independent and self-sufficient through their weaving, trading, buying and selling in the tourist markets. In various villages, widowed and single women have formed cooperatives designed to help them gain economic security and independence. In some cases, although not all by any means, young Mayan women find the institution of marriage less attractive than their ancestors did, preferring the freedom that their relatively new economic independence allows them.

The speed with which gender roles are changing in traditional Mayan society is a reflection of other changes in the customs and traditions of Mayan communities. Communities that had survived centuries with relatively little change are currently undergoing extensive transformations because of the social, political and economic reasons already mentioned. Traditional Mayan culture was based on agriculture, with some limited craft production and trade. Most Mayan communities were largely self-sufficient and, for this reason, were able to maintain their traditions without extensive interference. In this century various factors have forced changes among Mayan communities. A dwindling land supply (due to commercial-crop growth) and a growing population (possibly because of access to vaccines and antibiotics), have forced the Mayas away from a self-sufficient, agriculturally based existence. People are compelled to leave their communities to seek employment elsewhere. If they return, they bring outside influences with them. Mass media, which is mostly radio but increasingly includes television in those communities with electricity, has made its impact. The small *tiendas* (local stores) are packed with Coca-Cola, Fritos and cigarettes. The national schools have also affected Mayan culture, as the language of instruction is Spanish. The massive 1976 earthquake displaced thousands and brought more outsiders into Mayan communities. Most significant to the erosion of the Mayan way of life has been the political violence that forced a million Mayas to flee their communities to escape mostly military and paramilitary terrorism and brutality. Although a peace treaty between the guerrillas and the military was signed in 1996, the consequences of the violence still have widespread ramifications for the Mayas. For instance, some Mayan refugees who fled for their lives to Mexico during the 1970s and 1980s have returned under government protection, but they still find themselves victims of massacres and violence by the military and paramilitary groups.

All of these factors have contributed, on the one hand, to an erosion of Mayan cultural identity and, on the other hand, to a revitalization of the Mayan way of life. Mayan women play an extremely important role in the latter, providing the clay from which their tradition is molded. This is in the form of weaving and *traje*. *Traje* is not just clothing. It is an avowal of cultural distinction. To wear *traje* is to proclaim proudly that one is Maya and will continue to be Maya (Hendrickson, 1995). The Mayas today face perhaps one of the most difficult challenges to their cultural identity in 500 years. They are finding the solution through cultural venues, cultivating the study of Mayan languages, the Mayan calendar, Mayan literature, Mayan mythology and Mayan *costumbre*, which includes the use of *traje*. Although this is a central concern for a relatively reduced group of Mayan intellectuals, it is sparking interest and excitement among the young Mayan population who come into contact with this revitalization movement, and who perceive it as a way to reaffirm their ethnic identity. The future of Mayan cultural identity is in their hands.

FOLKLORE

Maximón

Maximón is a Mayan saint who is a blend of indigenous and Ladino characteristics, which gives him colorful attributes and a unique character. It is believed that Maximón evolved from the ancient deity called Mam, who was used to celebrate the Uayeb, a period of eight days between the old and new years. Mam, meaning grandfather, was symbolized by a piece of wood that was decorated for the event, then placed on a bench resting on a *petate* (woven straw mat). Gifts of food, moonshine and other trinkets were offered to him during this period to ensure a rich harvest and good fortune. At the end of the eight days, the piece of wood would be discarded without further ceremony (Mendelson, 1965).

The present-day Maximón is an important saint in Santiago Atitlán and a handful of other indigenous villages. He is also popular in the Ladino town of San Andrés Itzapa, in Quetzaltenango, and in Sololá and Chimaltenango, although he is not known in many other areas of Guatemala. Various legends are associated with his origins, mostly having to do with his double personality as protector of sexual virtue and abuser of the same. In Santiago Atitlán the story that the elders tell is that Maximón was first constructed by the deities as a guardian of morality on earth. But as he gained more and more power, he would disguise himself as a loved one and have sexual relations with males and females indiscriminately, thereby becoming the abuser of the very code that he was supposed to enforce (Castañeda-Medinilla, 1979). One oral history passed on by the elders is about two merchants who, due to the nature of their business, traveled frequently. They consequently left their wives alone for long periods of time. When one of the traders discovered that his wife was having an affair, he and his partner pretended to leave town but instead lay in wait for the adulterous pair. The husband then killed them by hanging. To escape accusation, the two merchant friends constructed a *palo de pito* (wooden doll) that produced whistling sounds in the air. Because the townspeople began to question the whereabouts of the merchant's wife, the merchants did not have time to finish the doll and left it without hands. When the leaders of the community arrived at the house, they found the strangled pair along with this strange, handless doll emitting eerie sounds. According to this legend, Maximón was born then as the protector of virgins and virtuous couples (Sanchiz Ochoa, 1993).

The Maximón of Santiago Atitlán is a piece of wood of about one and a half meters high. Another piece of wood, or perhaps a squash or pumpkin, forms the head, on top of which is placed a wooden mask. The wooden body is wrapped with rags and husks of corn, then dressed in a male suit that is typical of the region. Although he used to be brought out only during Holy Week, because of the numerous pilgrims, *brujos* (chamans) and tourists who visit Maximón in Santiago Atitlán, he sits in attendance all year long on his *petate* in the center of a room, surrounded by offerings of candles, *aguardiente* (moonshine), *pom* (incense) and cigarettes. Maximón's fondness for tobacco is well known, and his image is often represented while smoking a *puro* (handrolled cigarette). Those who have special petitions sacrifice a live chicken, while others leave gifts of moonshine, money or candles.

Maximón presides over Holy Week through the acting out of the Passion, Crucifixion and Resurrection of Christ. Like the eight days of Uayeb, this signifies the end of one natural cycle and the beginning of another. Every year on Holy Wednesday, a group of men carry Maximón to the municipal building, where he is placed among baskets of fruit that have been brought in from the coast for this purpose. At noon he is taken in a procession to a place outside of the church, where he is hung on a post. People offer him candles and incense while they pray. Finally, on Good Friday, Maximón is carried as part of the procession for the symbolic burial of Christ. But he is suddenly removed to be placed in a different home that will house him until Holy Week of the following year.

The parallels with Judas Iscariot are obvious, but this saint differs from representations of the traitor Judas in that he is not scorned or destroyed at the end of Holy Week. In fact, he is named Pedro (Peter) or Pedro Simón (Simon Peter), after the other apostle who abandoned Christ. The combination of Mam (grandfather) and Simón form the name of Maximón.

Maximón is a curious and unique saint in that he combines multiple contradictions, practicing good and evil at the same time. In the Christian context he is a traitor, but he is also capable of doing good. He is simultaneously a protector and an abuser of sexual virtue, which is why he is the patron saint of the virtuous and of prostitutes. Referring back to the legend described above, it seems that Maximón has a particular role in villages whose economies are based on trade and commerce. Because the men traditionally traveled frequently, it was necessary to have a saint to protect the virtue of the spouse left behind. Maximón seems to play diverse roles, involving sexuality, agrarian cycles and commerce (Sanchiz Ochoa, 1993).

In other towns where Maximón is venerated, such as San Lucas, Nahualá and Patzún, he takes on different characteristics. The rituals associated with him vary as well. The complexity of his personality is reflected in the numerous roles that he adopts; he can be Judas Iscariot, Pedro de Alvarado, Saint Andres, Saint Michael, Saint Peter or Mam, the ancient Mayan deity, all at once (Mendelson, 1965). In San Andrés Iztapa, a Ladino town, Maximón loses his indigenous character and becomes San Simón. There he is kept in a temple all year, cared for by a committee. This San Simón is a white mannequin with a thick moustache. He is dressed in a Western suit and sits in a chair on an elevated altar; the faithful must approach him by ascending the stairs. Yet generally worshipers do not differentiate between this San Simón and Maximón because, curiously, they represent the same saint. Large numbers of national and international visitors arrive yearly, especially for the feast of San Simón de Iztapa on October 28. With the presence of numerous prostitutes and vast quantities of moonshine, this festival becomes something of an orgy in honor of San Simón.

In recent decades Maximón has become a popular deity among the Garífuna population in Izábal on the eastern coast. The African Guatemalan population venerate him with African songs and dances to the rhythm of their traditional drums. How is it that Maximón has become such a celebrated saint among so many diverse populations? His popularity is attributed to the many who proclaim that he has executed miracles that have changed their lives. These miracles consist of the spiritual and material aspects of health, love and wealth. His amulets and talismans, especially the stone blessed by Maximón, are revered and carried to ward off evil spirits. For some the most fascinating aspect about Maximón is that he is venerated by the Mayas, the Ladinos, *mestizos* (mixed Spanish and Indian blood) from other countries, Westerners and Garífunas alike, representing a true transcultural blend of ethnic and racial sectors that seems to transcend divisions, if only for the moment, in a manner that is seldom achieved. In this lies, perhaps, the true magic of Maximón.

Nahuales (Animal Spirits)

Among the Indians of Guatemala and elsewhere in Latin America, there continues to exist the belief that human beings are accompanied through life by a kindred animal spirit, a *nahual*, although in some areas this has been replaced by the Christian concept of a guardian angel. However, the belief is still commonplace that at the moment a human is born, an animal comes into the world simultaneously to accompany and protect the human. The elders and the midwife of the community may know which animal is the *nahual* of the recently born, but they do not tell the child until s/he is older so that s/he will not be tempted to imitate the animal. Instead, the kinship between the human and the animal is supposed to develop naturally, and the human should acquire certain characteristics of his or her *nahual* as time transpires. So an individual may be aggressive or passive, nervous or calm, outgoing or shy, flamboyant or retiring, mischievous or serious, graceful or clumsy, all depending on the nature of the animal spirit. Individuals may also have certain physical attributes associated with their *nahual*, such as an ability to run, jump, swim, climb, sing, dig, hunt, fish and so on. In some areas it is believed that the individual in certain moments may assume the body of his or her *nahual*. They may fly through the air like a bird, leap over barriers like a deer or perform tasks that would not be possible in human form. This is consistent with the widespread beliefs and practices that the Spanish missionaries and conquistadors observed upon their arrival in the fifteenth and sixteenth centuries.

Documents from the eighteenth century reveal how Christianity had not been able to overcome the native belief system, part of which was a veneration and respect for animals. In 1770, Archbishop Cortes y Larraz recorded in a manuscript various practices of the Indians in villages that he visited in Guatemala. One of them included the rituals associated with the hunt. He described how the Mayas would ask permission of the deer spirit to kill one of the herd. He recorded the rituals associated with the killing, butchering and eating of the deer, which were all accompanied by prayer, candles and other signs of respect. The archbishop also recorded how the Mayas held special veneration for the images of saints that were accompanied by animals, such as Saint Francis, Saint James and Saint John, to the point that the priests in one diocese became concerned that the Mayas were worshiping the images of the animals rather than the image of the saint. Because of this, all images with animals were banished from the churches in the seventeenth century (Hurtado, 1971).

The archbishop also noted the many animal surnames of the Indians, such as del Caballo (of the horse), del Venado (of the deer), del Perro (of the dog), and so on. In contemporary villages and towns in the highlands, it is still common to find such names. However, it is not easy to discover the *nahual* of an individual. As the Mayan Nobel laureate Rigoberta Menchú states in her famous testimony, the *nahual* of a Maya remains a private secret that is not to be revealed to outsiders.

Mayan and Christian Folklore

When the Spanish arrived in Guatemala, they brought with them a crusader mentality that they had inherited from over 700 years of battling the Moors to reconquer Spain, to rid the country of the infidels and to claim it for the Christians. In this respect, it is significant that 1492 marks the expulsion of the Moors and Jews from Spain and the beginning of the invasion of the Americas by the Europeans. The conquistadors in the Americas vanquished the indigenous civilizations in the name of the Spanish monarchs and in the name of the Christian God, while claiming the spoils of war to enrich themselves. The missionaries who traveled with the conquistadors were zealous in assiduously instructing and assisting in the destruction of any manifestations of indigenous religions, be they images, altars, temples, sacrificial stones, urns, ornaments, codices or pictographic manuscripts. Thousands of documents describing the history, social customs and traditions of pre-Columbian civilizations were lost forever. Parallel to the massive destruction of artifacts, people and civilizations were the missionaries' efforts to convert the "pagans" and save their souls for Christ. However, many Spaniards did not believe that the Indians possessed souls, which meant that they need not be treated like humans. As Christian doctrine prohibited the use of humans as slaves, this led to the famous debate of the sixteenth century between the Indian defender, Fray Bartolomé de las Casas, and a Spaniard, Ginés de Sepúlveda. There was much at stake for both the Spaniards and the Indians in the Americas. If it was declared that the Indians did not possess souls and were therefore not human beings, they could be enslaved by the Spaniards and made to work their former lands and mines, which the Spaniards now controlled. The pope passed a papal bull in 1538 proclaiming that the Indians did possess souls and therefore could not be enslaved according to Christian doctrine. This was a blow to the Spanish colonizers, but the *encomienda* system, in which the Indians were put into feudal servitude, served almost the same purpose in exploiting the Indians as a labor force.

Catholic priests were set up in indigenous parishes. The Indians were forced to build Catholic Churches. The clergy oversaw the destruction of the "pagan" idols, substituting Catholic images in their place. The villages were named after a particular patron saint, which was housed and worshiped in the church. The *guachibales* and *cofradías* functioned as organizations in which the Indians venerated the patron saint or another image that they kept in their homes. The Catholic clergy, for the most part, was satisfied at the devotion that the Indians showed to the new Christian images. What many of them did not realize was that the Indians continued to worship their idols in secret while worshiping the Catholic ones publicly. They had also made their own substitutions. Each Catholic image was considered to have attributes of an indigenous deity or spirit. In essence, the image had changed its external form, but the "pagan" spirit was considered to reside in the image and perform the same functions as before the Christian onslaught.

In Guatemala the Spaniards conquered the capital of Quiché in 1524. The religious fusion of Mayan-Christian concepts and practices began at that time. Oral histories passed on through generations of Mayas and transcribed into written form demonstrate the interchangeable nature of Mayan deities and Christian saints. For instance, Mayan tales about the origin of corn mix and replace Mayan with Christian deities. In a legend from the Quiché of Nahualá-Ixtahuacán, the Mayan deities of thunder and lightning, the Chacs, are replaced by angels (Mondloch, 1982). Other tales involve the Lords of the Mountains, who own and oversee all the flora and fauna on the mountains, controlling the rains from within their domains in the earth (Thompson, 1954). If a Maya wants to cut down a tree or hunt an animal, he must make offerings and ask the Lords for permission; otherwise he will be punished. In some areas it is believed that the Lords, who take the form of Ladinos, have large plantations in the volcanoes and mountains. Surrounded by riches, they have the souls of the dead labor for them (Watanabe, 1992), similar to a Dantesque scene of hell.

In some tales the blend of Mayan and Christian mythologies is more obvious than in others. One legend tells of a poor, ill man who is deceived by a rich man and left to die in the mountains. But the Lords of the Mountains, taking pity on him, cure him, give him money and send him off as a rich man. When the rich man hears the story, he attempts to take advantage of the Lords by entering the forest and pretending to be sick. The Lords of the Mountains, who could look into the souls of mankind, were angered by this deceit. They punished the man by implanting a huge goiter on his throat. Here humility triumphs over greed and ambition.

In another tale a sorcerer is at work in the mountains. He attacks groups of merchants traveling between villages and cities. The sorcerer casts a spell over the merchants, making them fall asleep, and then robs them of everything they have. Numerous groups of armed men have tried to catch the thief to no avail. Finally, a group of young, confident men set out to rid the mountains of the thief. An old man joins them in the evening, and they reluctantly allow him to sleep on the outskirts of their camp. That night the sorcerer casts his spell and everyone falls asleep except for the old man. He attacks the thief, and a mighty battle ensues. When the old man tires, he calls out to the morning star, Santiago, which represents St. James, the Catholic warrior. The morning star turns into a resplendent vision of a soldier with a lance on a horse. The vision throws his lance to the ground and carries the thief high into the air, dropping him to be impaled on the lance.

In both of these tales good triumphs over evil due to the intervention of spirits. The role that the Lords of the Mountains in the first story play is quite similar to the one that a Catholic saint, St. James, plays in the second. In the first a sick, poor man is rewarded. In the second an old, seemingly feeble man triumphs. In both stories the evil man is punished (Mondloch, 1982).

This kind of religious syncretism in which Catholic saints take on attributes of Mayan deities is common among Mayas today. According to the stories told in Nahualá-Ixtahuacán, many of the Catholic saints lived as Lords of the Mountains until they were brought to the church in town to act as protectors of the village. Both Mayan deities and Catholic saints have the power to protect, to enrich or to punish. Pedro, a Mayan man who was severely injured when the tree he was chopping down fell on him in Santiago Atitlán attributed it to his lack of showing respect and gratitude for everything that the Lords had provided for him and his family (Shea, 1989). Sicknesses or natural calamities are considered punishments for some infringement, such as an unwillingness to serve in public projects.

In other tales the Christian element is not so obvious, but one may draw sociological parallels between the Ladino as oppressor and the Maya as the oppressed. A widely popular myth is about the Ladino spirit known as Juan Noj, or Juan el Gordo in some localities, who appears on horseback in remote areas and offers riches to men in return for their souls. Although it takes on numerous variations, this myth is widespread throughout the Mayan region. It is related by the Mam in Santiago Chimaltenango in Huehuetenango, by the Tzeltal of Zinacanatán in Chiapas, Mexico, by the Quiché of San Antonio Ilotenango and El Palmar, by the Tzutuhil of San Pedro la Laguna on Lake Atitlán and by the Chorti of Chiquimula. It has been suggested that the theme evolved from pre-Columbian beliefs in the Chorti area, which held that huge serpents lived in the volcanoes to enforce the tributes that the tribesmen paid to their chiefs. These images may have been replaced by the Ladino figure who enslaved the Indians in his feudal-like *encomienda* (Falla, 1971).

The belief is that Juan Noj represents *el mundo* (the world) and lives inside the volcano in a palace of silver and gold. His clothing and shoes are of silver and gold, although it is said that he also appears at times in the clothing of Tecúm-Umán, a Mayan warrior. He is both good and evil. He is good because he is responsible for bountiful crops, rain and other natural riches; He is bad because he is a usurer with cruel terms. Generally, he punishes the overly greedy or ambitious and rewards the poor. On occasion, however, he also enslaves the poor. He offers immense riches in return for a man's soul, and he protects the riches while the man is alive. In numerous stories, thieves attempt in vain to rob the riches, discovering snakes or spiders where the money, gold or silver should be. When the man dies, Juan Noj takes his soul to his kingdom to toil for him until the debt is paid. One variation has to do with the belief of the Mayas that the soul can temporarily leave the body while in life, causing illnesses. Thus the soul can be made to leave the body in life to pay the debt.

In one story Juan Noj makes a poor man rich, which causes envy in his rich *compadre*. The *compadre* also seeks out Juan Noj, who takes him to work in his mountain palace. His first task is to beat three pigs to death with a stick. One of them cries out not to be hit, as he is his *compadre*, the poor man who previously sold his soul to Juan Noj. In this tale, apparently, the soul left the body of the poor man in life to be transformed into one of Juan Noj's pigs. The rich man is able to leave but now has an enormous *huehuecho* (goiter) (Falla, 1971).

In this tale the poor and the rich man are punished alike, demonstrating the erratic nature of Juan Noj, who in some areas is seen as Satanás (Satan). There are numerous tales that demonstrate how Mayan and Christian beliefs have been fused into their own particular form of syncretized conceptions. It becomes apparent that the Christian deities were assigned roles that belonged to Mayan deities and vice versa, and that they play similar roles while wearing different masks.

CUISINE

Guatemalan cuisine may be divided into three categories: the typical foods of the Mayas in the highlands, the dishes of the Ladinos in the urban areas and the lowlands, and to a lesser extent, the African-influenced cuisine of the Garífuna in Livingston. The differences in cuisine are motivated to a large degree by the flora and fauna of geographic location. Cuisine becomes associated with ethnic identity. This is especially true of the Mayas, as they depend on their own crops and on what they trade in the markets for sustenance.

The main staple of the Mayan diet is maize, most of which they grow on their *milpas* (small plots of land). From ground maize the Mayan women create a paste that is patted to form round tortillas, which they heat on their *comals* (clay platters). The tortillas accompany most meals, and so the task is repeated two or three times daily. They are generally kept warm by being covered or wrapped in a *servilleta*. The women will frequently carry the warm tortillas out to the fields to serve lunch to their working men. Black beans are the other staple of the Mayan diet, and they are prepared in a variety of manners. They are served as a soup, as a fried-bean paste, with rice, as a purée and mixed in stews. Vegetables are plentiful due to the richness of the volcanic soil. Squash, tomatoes, hot chiles and peppers are common. Carrots, cabbage, beets, cauliflower, lettuce, chard, onion, garlic and leek are also popular, depending on geography and climatic conditions.

A popular dish in the Mayan highlands is *pepián*, a tasty chicken stew flavored by squash seeds, hot chiles, tomatillos and tomatoes. It is served on special occasions. Another dish is *pinol*, a chicken-flavored corn gruel. Other nutritious *caldos* (soups) that are made from vegetables and/or chicken stock help keep one warm in the cold highlands. *Atol*, a liquid gruel made from corn that may be served cold but is mostly served hot, also helps to take the chill out of the air. It is popular throughout Guatemala.

Tortillas and beans are also popular among Ladinos, as is *pepián*, which is made with beef in certain areas. Beef is much more commonplace in the urban areas than it is in the highlands. One popular dish is *carne asado*, a charcoal-broiled filet of beef. Guacamole, white country cheese, black beans and fried plantains accompany the *carne asado* to form a typical luncheon or dinner dish. Soups also may form part of the main meal. A common dish is *sopa de ajo*, a garlic soup with bread.

A popular meal in Guatemala City and other urban areas is *arroz con pollo chapina*, a chicken-rice dish that is flavored with onion, garlic, capers, carrots, tomatoes, peppers and a variety of vegetables in season. *Jocón*, chicken in a green sauce made from *pepitoria* (squash seeds), scallions, tomatillos, chile slices, sesame seeds and cilantro is another tasty dish. *Chojin* is a well-liked salad in Guatemala City and the surrounding towns. It is made with *chicharrones* (fried pork rinds) and mixed with onions, tomatoes, radishes, then flavored with mint and lemon juice. *Chiles rellenos* is another prevalent dish, consisting of peppers stuffed with pork or beef combined with carrots, tomatoes, onions and garlic, which are then coated with an egg mixture and fried in oil. *Tamales*, bits of chicken, pork, corn paste or potatoes steamed in banana leaves or foil, are eaten throughout Guatemala. *Mole*, a stew or dessert that may be mixed with chocolate, is commonplace. Cooked hen in chocolate sauce is quite popular, while fried plantains in chocolate sauce is a tasty dessert (Marks, 1985).

Plantains are green bananas that are eaten mostly in the cities and in the lowlands where they are grown. They can be prepared in numerous ways, and they are eaten as a vegetable or as a fruit. Fried plantains frequently accompany a breakfast of beans, tortillas and eggs. They can also be baked, cooked in sauces or syrups, stuffed, mashed and served as a pancake. They are popular as desserts. They can be prepared with honey and cinnamon-flavored syrups, put in an orange sauce topped with whipped cream, basted in a caramel syrup or served in rich chocolate sauces.

Fiambres are salads of cold meat and vegetables. They are prepared in large quantities for important events, especially All Saints' Day (November 1). They are platters of chicken, hen, sausage and tongue mixed with marinated vegetables such as carrots, cauliflower and green beans. They are laid on a bed of lettuce and garnished with olives, hard-boiled eggs, radishes, beets, cheese, onions and chiles.

Sweets are popular among Guatemalans. A variety of honeyed, candied and sugary desserts are prepared for special occasions. *Camote en dulce tina,* sweet potatoes cooked with plantains, cinammon sticks, honey, milk, butter and vanilla, are topped with raisins. They are popular in Antigua. Rice cakes, honey crisps, sugared figs, *buñuelos* (fried dumplings in honey) and cinnamon custards are examples of some of the sweets that are consumed among the populace. These are eaten mostly in the urban areas. The *borracho* (drunkard) is a popular dish made from eggs, sugar, cinnamon, flour and—the essential ingredient—rum. It is favored among the upper classes in Guatemala City.

Guatemalans consume a variety of tasty alcoholic drinks. One is *rompopo,* a drink made from sweetened, condensed milk, egg yolks and rum. Another is *chicha,* wine made from a variety of fruits such as apples, peaches, and cherries. It is mixed with cinnamon, sugar and white rum. It must be bottled and stored for several months to ferment. In Cobán, a sugarcane drink known as *boj* is popular.

Guatemalans in the highlands and in the principal cities generally do not consume much fish, with some exceptions in those villages near rivers or lakes. In Santiago, Atitlán, for instance, *patín* is made from toasted freshwater minnows cooked with tomatoes and hot chiles. However, in the coastal areas on the Pacific and the Caribbean, there is a rich assortment of seafood dishes, especially in the Caribbean city of Livingston. Sea bass, flounder, red snapper, tarpon and other varieties of fish are prepared in numerous ways. Many dishes are flavored with milk from coconuts, which are common to this tropical region. Sautéed fish in tomato, onion, garlic, bay leaves and other spices is commonplace, as is fish sautéed in coconut milk and cooked with peppers, tomatoes and celery. Soups composed of fish mixed with tomatoes, onions, celery, cilantro, carrots and black pepper are daily fare. Shrimp dishes are also quite popular, especially garlic-shrimp dishes and breaded shrimp. In the Pacific port of San José, shark steaks are marinated in lime or lemon juice and then fried in corn oil. *Savalo* (tarpon) is caught daily off the coast of Livingston. It is made into a hash with potatoes or *huisquil* (chayote), carrots, tomatoes, onions, pepper and vinegar. *Seviche* is composed of shellfish, shrimps and, at times, squid. It is chilled in lemon juice and mixed with tomatoes, onion, mint, parsley and hot chiles. *Tapado* is a popular seafood stew made of shrimp, crabs and different kinds of fish, mixed with green peppers, tomatoes, onions, plantains and coconut milk (Marks, 1985).

Guatemalan cuisine varies according to region, with a creative assortment of dishes that combines the basic foods common to the area in different ways. Some are standard fare throughout Guatemala, such as tortillas and beans.

The prevalence of others, such as the dishes flavored with coconut milk, is determined by factors such as geographic location, local climate and soil conditions.

REFERENCES

Castañeda-Medinilla, José. "Maximón, un caso de magia imitativa." *Guatemala Indígena* 14.3–4 (1979): 131–42.

Chicas, Rendón, Otto, Gaitán Alfaro, and Héctor Gaitán Alfaro. *Recetario y Oraciones Secretas de Maximón*. Guatemala City: Nueva Guatemala de la Asunción, 1995.

Falla, Ricardo. "Juan El Gordo: visión indígena de su explotación." *Estudios Centroamericanos* 26.268 (1971): 98–107.

Fischer, Edward F., and R. Mckenna Brown, eds. *Maya Cultural Activism in Guatemala*. Austin: University of Texas Press, 1996.

Hendrickson, Carol. "Handmade and Thought-Woven: The Construction of Dress and Social Identity in Tecpan Guatemala." Ph.D. diss. University of Chicago, 1986.

———. *Weaving Identities*. Austin: University of Texas Press, 1995.

———. "Women, Weaving and Education in Maya Revitalization." In Edward F. Fischer and R. McKenna Brown, eds., *Maya Cultural Activism*. Austin: University of Texas Press, 1996. 156–64.

Hurtado, Juan José. "Algunas ideas sobre el culto de los animales y el nahualismo en el siglo XVIII." *Guatemala Indígena* 6.4 (1971): 176–83.

Juarros, Juan Domingo. *Compendio de la historia de la Ciudad de Guatemala*. Guatemala City: Tip. Nacional, 1937.

Luján Muñoz, Luis. *Tradiciones navideñas de Guatemala*. Guatemala City: Cuadermos de la tradición guatemalteca, 1981.

Marks, Copeland. *False Tongues and Sunday Bread: A Guatemalan and Mayan Cookbook*. New York: M. Evans and Company, Inc., 1985.

Meléndez, Ofelia Columba Déleon. *La Feria de Jocotenango en la ciudad de guatemala: una aproximación histórica y etnográfica*. Guatemala City: Editorial Universitaria, 1983.

Mendelson, E. Michael. *Los Escándalos de Maximón*. Guatemala City: Seminario de Integracón Social Guatemalteca, 1965.

Mondloch, James. "Sincretismo religioso maya-cristiano en la tradición oral de una communidad quiché." *Mesoamérica* 3.3 (1982): 107–23.

Otzoy, Irma. "Maya Clothing and Identity." In Edward F. Fischer and R. McKenna Brown, eds., *Maya Cultural Activism*. Austin: University of Texas Press, 1996. 141–55.

Pardo, J. J., Pedro Zamora, and Luis Luján. *Guía de Antigua Guatemala* (Guide to Antigua Guatemala), 3rd ed. Guatemala City: Editorial José de Pineda Ibarra, 1969.

Quintanilla Meza, Carlos Humberto. *La semana santa en Antigua Guatemala*. La Antigua, Guatemala: Consejo Nacional para la Protección de La Antigua Guatemala, 1989.

Sanchiz Ochoa, Pilar. "Sincretismo de ida y vuelta: el culto de San Simón en Guatemala." *Mesoamérica* 14.26 (1993): 253–66.

Shea, Maureen. Oral interviews with various Mayas during the summers of 1988–1993.

Smith, Kenneth W. "Todos los Santos: Spirits, Kites, and Courtship in the Guatemalan Maya Highlands." *Folklore Americano* 26 (1978): 49–58.

Sperlich, Norbert, and Elizabeth Katz Sperlich. *Guatemalan Backstrap Weaving*. Norman: University of Oklahoma Press, 1980.

Thompson, Donald E. *Mayan Paganism and Christianity: A History of the Fusion of Two Religions*. New Orleans, LA: Middle American Research Institute, 1954.

Watanabe, John M. *Maya Saints and Souls in a Changing World*. Austin: University of Texas Press, 1992.

Wilentz, Gay. *Binding Cultures*. Bloomington: Indiana University Press, 1992.

Woman from Nahualá, with baby. Courtesy of R. C. Finch.

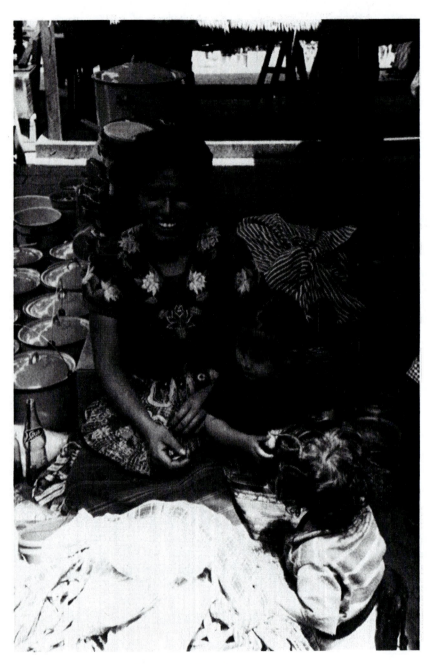

In the market, Antigua. Courtesy of Rosa Howard.

Marketplace, Antigua. Courtesy of Rosa Howard.

Mayan woman weaving on backstrap loom.
Courtesy of Rosa Howard.

Mayan woman carrying child while washing clothes at the local *pila* in Antigua. Courtesy of Rosa Howard.

Mayan women washing clothes at the local *pila*, Antigua. Courtesy of Rosa Howard.

Mayan woman vendor selling wares in the central part of Antigua. Courtesy of Rosa Howard.

Kite festival in Sacatepéquez for the town's All Saint's Day. Kites carry messages to communicate with the dead or petitions to God. CIDA Photo: Brian Atkinson.

Beginning of the traditional dance that tells the story of the Spanish Conquest during the festival at Todos Santos. CIDA Photo: Benoit Aquin.

Ceremony for refugees at the Guatemalan border. CIDA Photo: Peter Bennett.

Music blasts from busses like this one, which are the typical form of local transportation in Guatemala. Courtesy of Rosa Howard.

Example of an indoor patio in a colonial-style house. Courtesy of Rosa Howard.

Man of San Juan Atitán. Courtesy of R. C.
Finch.

Young Mam Maya man of Todos Santos Cuchumatán, at the ancient ceremonial
site above the town. Courtesy of R. C. Finch.

Man and woman from Sololá selling vegetables at the Chichicastenango market. Courtesy of R. C. Finch.

Native Maya musicians at Chichicastenango. Courtesy of R. C. Finch.

Mam Maya children in the town of Todos Santos Cuchumatán. Courtesy of R. C. Finch.

Typical thatched roof Maya house in the Altos Cuchumatanes Mountains near Nebaj. Courtesy of R. C. Finch.

Quiché Maya girl at stone idol near Chichicastenango. Courtesy of R. C. Finch.

Two happy young Maya girls on the plaza of
Antigua. Courtesy of R. C. Finch.

Ixil Maya family in Nebaj. Courtesy of R. C. Finch.

4

Broadcasting and Print Media

THERE HAS BEEN limited development of broadcasting and print media in the Central American nations due to censorship, lack of resources and a large, illiterate, and impoverished, agrarian population. Newspapers are mostly produced in the principal cities with little circulation in the rural areas. In Guatemala, where about 5 million people are Mayas living in the countryside, the leading newspapers are printed in Spanish and circulated almost exclusively in Guatemala City. In the outlying rural or coastal areas where many people communicate through an oral tradition, radio and television are a much more prevalent form of communication in areas where there is electricity and among those who can afford them. However, newspapers are the most developed form of media, followed by radio, then television.

The major newspapers in Guatemala City are *Prensa Libre*, with a circulation of about 68,000, and *El Gráfico* with about 60,000. Other major newspapers with much less circulation are *La Hora* (about 20,000) *Diario de Centroamerica* (about 15,000). *Siglo Veintiuno*, and *La República* have even less circulation. Even in this limited nucleus, however, newspapers have been severely curtailed by official censors who have traditionally monitored what is published. There is institutional retaliation in the form of shutting down opposition newspapers or imprisoning journalists and publishers. There is also unofficial, brutal retaliation against those who write or publish articles that expose repression or corruption on the part of the government, the military or the dominant private sector.

From the 1960s to about 1996, the years of guerrilla insurgency and army retaliation, journalism in Guatemala was an extremely dangerous profession.

Hundreds of journalists were imprisoned, kidnapped and beaten for exposing corruption, human-rights violations and repression by the authoritarian regimes. Seventy-nine journalists were "disappeared" or murdered. One was Jorge Carpio Nicolle, the editor of *El Gráfico*. He was assassinated by a dozen armed men who attacked his vehicle as he was traveling to a political meeting of his center-right party in July 1993. The government assumed the official position that ordinary criminals committed the murder, but family members and international human-rights groups are certain that it was politically motivated. After the peace accord was signed in 1996, the violence continued but now in the form of organized crime. Criminals formed alliances with corrupt army or police officers to participate in kidnapping, assassinations, drug trafficking and auto-theft rings. Journalists who reported these corrupt activities suffered repercussions that were officially classified as common crimes, although it was apparent to most that the retaliations were connected to their profession. The violence has led to a culture of silence in which the most controversial incidents that involve the state are barely reported. A vivid, graphic example was when President Jorge Serrano Elías shut down the government on May 25, 1993. In a coup he declared himself president for a second term. With strict censorship in effect, *Siglo Veintiuno* still appeared in the newspaper stalls the next day; the front page and most other pages were blacked out, with the exception of commercial advertisements. This symbolized the blackout of any opposition voices.

Nonetheless, with an end to overt government control of the media, there has been some progress made in allowing debate and the discussion of topics that were once forbidden. Improvements can be seen in the role of the press in the postwar era, the role of universities in providing professional schooling for journalists, the conduct and responsibilities of journalists, the effect of self-censorship on objective reporting, and the role of the press in reporting and raising awareness among the populace about the peace accords. Some journals and newspapers have experimented with innovative formatting and styles in conferring information, such as the magazine *La Crónica* (founded in 1987) and the daily newspapers *Siglo Veintiuno* (created in 1990) and *elPeriódico* (established in 1996).

Although there is less overt government control of the press since the 1996 peace accords, there is still an intolerant attitude toward the news media. This contributes to an atmosphere of fear and mistrust among journalists that causes self-censorship. This tense situation in which most Guatemalan journalists live has divided their ranks. Whereas other Latin American nations have one or two united journalists' organizations, Guatemala has seven, which are frequently in conflict with each other. This makes it more difficult to present a united front in opposing government or military censorship and repression. Also, because there are few professional journalism schools, amateur journalists traditionally depended on the knowledge and expertise that their editors could provide them. When editors were silenced or disappeared, younger journalists were left with little opportunity to acquire professional training. This has affected future generations of reporters. However, it seems that access to the Internet is filling the void and helping journalists acquire a sense of what professional journalism is about.

In recent years journalists have made efforts to include more multiethnic and multilingual aspects of Guatemalan culture, and articles in Mayan languages are published at times in *Siglo Veintiuno* and *La Hora*. However, these positive measures by the news media to reach the marginalized sectors of the population have been minimal, and the inclusion of indigenous languages in most of the media has yet to be addressed. Regardless, even such limited moves to advocate a more pluralistic, inclusive society have been perceived as threats to the status quo, and numerous journalists, radio broadcasters, and stations have been attacked. Many reporters who have been beaten or threatened have fled into exile.

As in many Latin American countries where the majority population is illiterate, radio programs have a widespread audience, especially in the rural areas. Even for those able to read, few journals reach the outlying rural regions. Oral broadcasts are much more accessible to an uneducated population, and numerous stations compete with each other for a diverse public. Many impoverished families have a radio or access to one at a local grocery store, *cantina* (bar) or at the homes of economically better-off family members. Traditionally, radio programs in Guatemala have concentrated on entertainment rather than on education. People have become immersed in the soap operas, talk shows and popular music that is broadcast on the national radio stations. In the past decade some radio stations have injected cultural or political commentaries into their transmittals. Some have broadcasts in a Mayan language, focusing on Mayan concerns and cultural questions.

Because radio and television have predominantly focused on entertainment rather than on information, they have been less vulnerable to attacks of a political nature. However, four major news networks provide information, and radio personnel have not escaped repercussions. Two staff members of *Radio campesina* were murdered in 1997, and another station, *La Voz de Petén*, was set on fire.

A Mexican private monopoly controls most television in Guatemala. Local channels that broadcast in the rural areas are embryonic and lack development. The Ministry of Education oversees Channel 5, which was once controlled by the army, but it lacks the resources to develop it into an effective mode of communication. In addition, most Guatemalans in the rural areas cannot afford a television even if they have access to electricity. In general, Guatemalan television is the weakest in Central America (International Institute for Democracy and Electoral Assistance).

There also exists an economic censorship where campaigns are conducted to withdraw the advertising that funds the publication of newspapers. Although this has not been successful in shutting down major newspapers such as *Prensa Libre*, it has managed to shut down less economically viable media outlets. Recently a government-led boycott attempted to shut down the newspaper *elPeriódico* and the magazine *La Crónica*, claiming that the journals were biased against the government. In April 1999 a radio show called *Hoy por Hoy* (Right Now) began broadcasting scandalous reports about certain journalists. Suspecting the involvement of the government, the relatively new *elPeriódico* sent out a team of investigative journalists and discovered that the program had indeed been created by the president's special adviser. So although improvements have been made, a contentious relationship between the press and the government still exists. However, that a newspaper is taking an active role in investigating government involvement in slander is indicative of a new openness.

The history of journalism in Guatemala has been grim. Hopes that conditions would improve after the peace accords of 1996 have barely materialized. This is apparent in the international condemnation of the lack of press freedom in Guatemala, which was expressed by directors and publishers of Latin American media in April 1997, and by the international Media Foundation in March 1997. The Guatemalan government needs to change its attitude and actions toward the press. The press needs to gain economic independence from the government and advertisers, and it needs to establish better educational opportunities for journalists to help them become objective reporters. Much depends on the future governments of Guatemala.

REFERENCES

Arana, Ana. "Attacks on the Press 1995." *The Americas*. Committee to Protect Journalists Publications Index: CRT Website, 1996. Available at http://www/cpj.org/pubs/attacks95/att95americas.html.
Ethiel, Nancy. "The Robert R. McCormick Tribune Foundation." *MTF Journalism 1994 Annual Report*. Available at http://rrmtt.org/journalism/jchap94.htm.
Fitzgerald, Mark. "Unprecedented Independence." *Editor and Publisher* 128.27 (July 1995). Available at www.northernlight.com.

Interiano, Carlos. *Comunicación, periodismo y paz en Guatemala.* Guatemala City: Universidad de San Carlos, 1996.

International Institute for Democracy and Electoral Assistance. "The Challenge of the Media in Guatemala." Available at http://www.intidea.se/publications/Guatemala/engguat-9media.html.

Smeets, Marylene. "Speaking Out: Postwar Journalism in Guatemala and El Salvador." Committee to Protect Journalists Publication Index. Available at http://www.cpj.org/dangerous/spring99/guatemala11august99.html.

Villatoro, Eduardo P., and Marco Tulio Barrios Reina, et al. *Comisión de Libertad de Prensa de la Asociación de Periodistas de Guatemala, Report on Press Freedom.* Guatemala City: Inter-American Commission on Human Rights Organization of American States, August 10, 1998. Available at http://www.ifex.org/alert.00003535.html.

5

Cinema

UNTIL RECENTLY, the film industry scarcely existed in Central America. In Guatemala a documentary film entitled *Vamos patria a caminar* (Onwards My Country, 1983) was produced during the 1980s by Cinematografía de Guatemala, a small filmmaking company. But until the 1990s no major feature film had ever been produced in Guatemala, largely due to its long history of censorship under dictatorship and its lack of institutional support for the arts. However, *El silencio de Neto* (The Silence of Neto, 1993), a major motion picture by Guatemalan producer, director and screenwriter Luis Argueta, indicates that Guatemala is ready to venture into the international film industry. It features an all-star cast that includes the well-known, U.S.-Latino actress Eva Tamargo Lemus.

El silencio de Neto is the story of a boy being raised in the upper classes of Guatemala during the turbulent period of the 1950s. The background events have to do with the revolutionary presidency of Jacobo Arbenz Guzmán, which was the first attempt to address Guatemala's principal socioeconomic, political problem: the inequity of land distribution. In his land-reform program Arbenz Guzmán appropriated all the untilled land of the wealthy elite and of the United Fruit Company and distributed it to landless peasants.

The young Neto (played by a Guatemalan schoolboy, Oscar Javier Almengor) observes these events while growing up in the beautiful city of Antigua. The viewer experiences various culturally rich Guatemalan traditions. The natural beauty of the land and the spectacular volcanoes that surround Antigua are represented in the film in a haunting fashion, and the artistically woven plot takes precedence over the political messages, which filter in through the radio broadcasts of *Radio Liberación* and in conversations among the adults. Yet the silence of the young protagonist, Neto, is representative of the silence of all Guatemalans during their unspeakably brutal history. The movie represents an effort to ensure that this silence is not repeated. Director Argueta has stated that he wanted to show a Guatemala that was not the stereotypical vision of a "banana republic" enmeshed in guerrilla turmoil, which is the most common image that the world has of his country, and to show that Guatemala "laughs, suffers, sings, and cries—a vital and intense country" (*The Silence of Neto*, 1999). From the reaction of the Guatemalan public and international film critics, it appears that Argueta has succeeded in opening the doors for the Guatemalan film industry.

It is too dangerous to film in Guatemala, so numerous movies, documentaries, and docudramas have been made in Mexico, Nicaragua, the United States and Europe about the turbulent and terrible years following the Arbenz Guzmán overthrow of 1954. A full-length major feature that won international acclaim was *El Norte* (The North, 1983). U.S. filmmakers Gregory Nava and Anna Thomas filmed the portion of the movie that represents Guatemala in Chiapas, Mexico, because of the similar natural setting and the Mayan population. Although less dangerous than filming it in Guatemala, they still ran into problems with the Mexican military and the film was almost confiscated, but the filmmakers managed to have it spirited out of the country.

El Norte is a trilingual movie that is divided chronologically into three parts, which take place in Guatemala, Mexico and the United States. The actors speak Mayan, Spanish and English. It is the story of Guatemalan Mayas who flee the scorched-earth tactics of the army that massacred their loved ones and destroyed their villages. In the movie, after the murder of their parents by the military, a brother and sister (Enrique, played by the Mexican actor David Villalpande, and Rosa, played by the Mexican actress Zaide Silvia Gutierrez) travel through the mountains into Mexico. They eventually make their way to Los Angeles. The voyage is fraught with dangers, and the naive protagonists seek strength in each other to survive encounters with unscrupulous "coyotes" (people who arrange illegal border crossings but frequently rob refugees and abandon them to their fate, often death), the Migra (the U.S. Immigration and Naturalization Service), and even hordes of rats. When they finally reach the mythical north, Los Angeles, they find that it is not quite the land of opportunity that was depicted in the *Good Housekeeping* magazines that their godmother kept back in their Guatemalan village. Once again they must overcome a series of cultural, economic and political obstacles to survive. Perhaps the real strength of the movie lies in its ability to contrast the cultural realities that refugees such as Rosa and Enrique face. They hold on to their Mayan identities while attempting to assimilate into the dominant culture. They learn to speak English and to dress like the North Americans in their struggle for survival. Director Nava has called the movie a journey through cultural layerings, and perhaps its success may be attributed to its sensitive treatment of the theme of understanding someone from another culture (Benamou, 1984).

El Norte is a moving, convincing account of the dilemma of desperate refugees who must flee their countries to escape death. They are not welcome and cannot survive in impoverished Mexico. They face the U.S. authorities' discrimination and harassment. They face the U.S. public's ignorance and indifference. Perhaps this last barrier is the ultimate obstacle that cannot be overcome. Rosa's final speech on her deathbed is a sorrowful tale of dispossessed emigrants who are not welcome anywhere and can only find a home in death.

Also produced in 1983 was the documentary film *When the Mountains Tremble*. U.S.-based, independent filmmakers Pamela Yates and Tom Sigel wanted to make a movie that told the story of events that occurred in Guatemala during the late 1970s and early 1980s. No such movie had ever been made, principally because of government-sponsored censorship and fear of reprisals. Instead of acting as intermediaries themselves, Yates and Sigel featured Rigoberta Menchú as the narrator who tells her story, the same narrated in her testimony, *I, Rigoberta Menchú*. Menchú's story is filmed in isolation in a film studio. It is interspersed with footage that Yates and Sigel filmed in Guatemala that documents military repression of the Mayas. What lends this film its unique character is that Yates and Sigel, conveying interest in military maneuvers in what the army considered the guerrilla infested highlands, were able to travel with the military and film scenes from their vehicles. They were also successful in convincing the guerrillas that the film would be useful in educating the U.S. public about the reasons for their insurgency. Hence the guerrillas allowed them to film maneuvers and scenes of daily life in their camps, which does away with the common portrayal of a guerrilla force composed only of Marxist foreigners. Many of the combatants filmed are Mayas, speaking about the significance of the revolutionary struggle in their own languages. The juxtaposition of scenes filmed with the military and the guerrillas is highly effective, mostly in discrediting military claims that they are fighting a Soviet-inspired communist insurgency.

Although Menchú narrates parts of the film, it soon becomes apparent that the events of the film are not seen through her eyes. There is another, more privileged eye: the eye of the camera. Yates and Sigel often maneuver the camera from military vehicles. Menchú would not have been allowed to set foot in such a vehicle; more than likely she would have been killed. In light of this, the isolation in which she is filmed acquires symbolic, even ominous dimensions. Although the film is openly partial toward the cause of the rebels, and the filmmakers admit that they did not attempt to achieve objectivity, their footage of the massacres of the Mayas is real. This reminds the public that what they are viewing is not fiction.

There are numerous other documentaries about the genocide against the Mayas during in the 1970s and 1980s, their forced relocation into "model villages" and the coerced participation of Mayan men into "civil patrols," their flight into the jungles of Ixcán and Mexico, and their return to their native land in 1997 after the signing of the peace treaty in 1996. The titles of many of these videos reveal the tragedy that motivated the filmmakers to bring attention to the plight of the Mayas: *Guatemala: A Journey to the End of Memories* (1986); *Guatemala: Caminos del silencio* (Guatemala: Roads of Silence, 1987); *The Long Road Home* (1992); *Resistir para vivir* (Struggling for Our Lives, 1991); *Todos Santos: The Survivors* (1989); *Winds of Memory* (1992); *Broken Silence: Rigoberta Menchú* (1992); and on a more hopeful note, *Tejedoras del futuro* (Weaving the Future, 1988).

REFERENCES

Benamou, Catherine. "El Norte." *Cine Si-New Latin American Cinema* (Fall 1984): 26–31.
Burton, Julianne. *Cinema and Social Change in Latin America: Conversations with Filmmakers*. Austin: University of Texas Press, 1986.
Fried, Jonathan. "*When the Mountains Tremble.*" *Areíto* 9–10 (1983–1984): 60–61.
King, John. *Magical Reels: A History of Cinema in Latin America*. London: Verso, 1990.
Ranucci, Karen, and Julie Feldman, eds. *A Guide to Latin American, Caribbean, and U.S. Latino-Made Film and Video*. Lanham, MD: The Scarecrow Press Inc., 1998.
Schnitman, Jorge A. *Film Industries in Latin America*. Norwood, NJ: Ablex, 1984.
Shea, Maureen. "*When the Mountains Tremble* and *I, Rigoberta Menchú*: Documentary Film and Testimonial Literature in Latin America." *Film Criticism* 18.2 (Winter 1994): 3–14.
The Silence of Neto. Available at http://members.aol.com/tikalan/arrival.htm (10/07/99).

6

Literature

GUATEMALAN LITERATURE has a long, divided cultural history. Its roots in an indigenous past became submerged during the Spanish invasion and 500 years of domination by the invaders and the Ladino intellectual elite. Although the contrast between the cultural traditions and beliefs of the majority Mayan population and that of the Ladinos distinguishes Guatemalan literature from the literature of other Latin American countries, it shares certain characteristics with its Central American neighbors. Because of the high rate of illiteracy among the general population, which is especially high among those countries with a large population of indigenous or African-descent residents, literature has not been a widespread cultural phenomenon in Central America. In Guatemala it has been estimated that in the mid-1970s, 80 percent of the rural population could not read or write (Nyrop, 1983). The estimated illiteracy rate was even higher for rural indigenous women. In addition, the language barriers between the indigenous population and the intellectual elite who produce literature have been vast. Historically, there has been very little institutional support at a regional or national level to encourage reading and writing among the general populace, either in their native language or in Spanish. In these circumstances only those literate in the middle or upper classes, which means mostly Ladino or White men, are able to write. Because of the scarcity of publishing houses only the best-known writers were published and became recognized. A major problem has been the lack of economic development among the Central American nations, which have remained in the hands of the traditional, oligarchic, landowning elite. This maintains the area's dependent status and relegates it to a subregion, in contrast to South American countries such as Brazil, Uruguay and Argentina, which diversified their economies and began developing their infrastructure, with attention paid to creating publishing houses, book dealers, and print media.

In Central America, with some exceptions, literature in the late nineteenth and early twentieth centuries continued to reflect the nostalgia of the upper classes for the customs and traditions of their elite status. This *costumbrista* (based on customs) literary mode and a preference for an ornamental, poetic style imitated European models. It had little to do with the Central American cultural realities that the majority of the population experienced. Although this has changed in some respects, who typically writes and reads literature in Central America is still determined by colonial practices of privilege and domination. As Guatemalan writer Arturo Arias puts it, conscientious intellectuals write not for the masses who cannot read; rather, they write to describe to the elite minority the conditions of the majority of the people in their countries who are otherwise kept marginalized and silenced (Arias, 1995). There are some recent exceptions among the indigenous population. Some have produced works through oral testimonies or through written texts. And although they are few, a growing number of Mayan intellectuals are intent on making their voices heard.

In this century various intellectuals from privileged or semiprivileged classes have associated themselves with different rural and urban sectors among the peasants and workers. The literature of these intellectuals reveals a class consciousness that clearly sympathizes with the underclasses. The *testimonio* (testimonial or testimonial novel), a vehicle through which the illiterate or marginalized sectors may speak, is an important forum for the Indians and women of different races, ethnicities or classes. But Central American writers who evoke the conditions of oppression that the majority of the population suffers risk their lives by incurring the wrath of the dominant governmental forces, which are supported by both the military and the paramilitary death squads. Numerous writers have been assassinated for expressing their dissent through literature or other venues. For this reason it has been said that a culture of silence exists in Central America in which the voices of the majority of the population have been suppressed. Under these conditions it is surprising that so many literary masterpieces have been produced in Central America.

Another factor that differentiates Central American from South American literature is the proximity of the United States, whose long history of invasion and intervention in its neighboring countries is a central theme in numerous

Central American works. The creation of the Panama Canal, the long domination of the United Fruit Company at the beginning of the twentieth
century and the incursions of U.S. interests and force into what they considered the "banana republics" initiated a long tradition of economic domination by the United States. Numerous U.S. presidents have supported the
immensely wealthy, oligarchic, Latin American dynasties that produced the
fanatical dictators that would plague Central America through much of its
painful history in this century. This is the subject of many novels, short
stories and poems. The lack of interest among those in power to develop the
natural resources of their respective countries and create an industrial infrastructure that would grant them some economic autonomy left the Central
American countries dependent on a cash economy, which is based almost
solely on monocultural crop exportation. Since the cash resources stayed in
the hands of the wealthy, this left a growing, immense gap between a handful
of very wealthy autocrats and masses of terribly impoverished residents. This,
in turn, led to revolutionary violence. The subsequent repercussions that
further alienated and impoverished most of the people were again the subject
of many Central American texts. Finally, the violence unleashed by natural
disasters—earthquakes, hurricanes, volcanoes, floods and draughts—as well
as the exuberant and spectacular beauty of its rich jungles, forests, mountains,
volcanoes, rivers and streams that are inhabited by all varieties of wildlife,
combined to inspire unique literary creations.

Among Central American countries Guatemala has the longest, richest
literary tradition. It stems from pre-Columbian or colonial texts penned in
Mayan hieroglyphic writing. Although the Spaniards destroyed thousands of
Mayan codices, partial histories survived through an oral tradition. Other
hieroglyphic documents went underground to emerge in a transformed state
decades or centuries later. The most significant is the *Popol Vuh*, or the *Mayan
Book of Counsel.* The royal Quiché rulers created the alphabetic version of
the *Popol Vuh* during the mid-1600s in the town of Quiché. In the text they
mention that they are working during the reign of the Christian God, but
they say that their own gods knew and saw everything. It is possible that,
threatened by the overzealousness of certain Catholic priests, the authors of
the alphabetic *Popol Vuh* hid the original to keep it from being destroyed. It
has never been found (Tedlock, 1985).

An alphabetic copy of the manuscript in the Quiché language was un-
earthed between 1701 and 1703 by Francisco Ximénez, a Dominican friar
who was serving as parish priest in the town of Chichicastenango. He made
a copy of the text and translated it into Spanish. It is the only existing copy

of the original alphabetic *Popol Vuh*. It subsequently made its way to Guatemala City and Europe, was translated into various languages, and eventually ended up in the Newberry Library of Chicago in 1911.

The *Popol Vuh* is an epic rich in Mayan Quiché mythology, cosmology and conceptual worlds that tells the story of the creation of humankind. It begins by describing the dilemmas and difficulties of the gods as they decide on the material from which they should shape humans. Their initial attempts at using monkeylike creatures, then mud, then wood all fail. They are finally successful when they settle on corn, the most important nutrient for the Mayas. The creation story is interrupted by a lengthy series of tales about the adventures of two sets of twins, descendants of the gods, who are experts at a Mesoamerican ball game. The first set of twins is defeated and sacrificed by the lords of Xibalba, the underworld. The second set becomes the "hero twins," as they take on the dark forces of Xibalba. The "hero twins" meet a series of challenges that the evil lords of Xibalba create. The "hero twins" persevere through ingenuity, persistence and bravery. They eventually beat the lords at the all-determining Mesoamerican ball game. This signifies the triumph of the sky-earth gods of Quiché over the underworld (Tedlock, 1985).

The stories told in the *Popol Vuh* are connected to Mayan beliefs and practices, including the Mayan calendar of cyclical time and the profound symbology that involves the spiritual dimensions of the natural world and beyond. The *Popol Vuh* deeply influenced Guatemalan contemporary literature. Its mythological and cultural dimensions can be found in such important works as Miguel Angel Asturias' *El señor presidente* (Mr. President, 1946) and *Hombres de maíz* (Men of Maize, 1949), Rigoberta Menchú's testimony, *Me llamo Rigoberta Menchú y así me nació la conciencia* (I, Rigoberta Menchú, 1984), Gaspar Pedro González's *La otra cara* (A Mayan Life, 1992) and *El retorno de los mayas* (The Return of the Mayas, 1998) to mention only a few.

Other important Mayan texts are the *Anales de los Kaqchikeles* (Annals of the Kaqchikels), which narrates the history of the Kaqchikels in their language shortly after the invasion of the Spaniards, the *Rabinal Achí*, a drama in Quiché that represents the struggle between the Quiché Mayas of Rabinal and Gumarcaaj to gain control over the region of Zamaneb in the twelfth century, and *El libro de Chilam Balam* (The Book of Chilam Balam), which recounts the anguish of the Mayas in the face of the Spanish onslaught. All of these works continue to be studied by anthropologists, linguists and ethnographers, many of them Mayas. These works have influenced various contemporary dramatic and literary representations.

On the other side of the cultural divide, it is important to mention the history of the conquest that a Spanish conquistador, Bernal Díaz del Castillo, wrote. Díaz del Castillo was one of the soldiers of Hernán Cortés, who invaded and defeated the Aztecs in their capital, Tenochtitlán, in 1521. As an elderly man, Díaz del Castillo moved to what is now Antigua, Guatemala, where one can still view the ruins of his dwelling. In response to other chronicles and histories that portrayed the conquest of Mexico as executed by the heroism of a single man, Hernán Cortés, Díaz del Castillo completed his *Historia verdadera de la conquista de Nueva España* (The True History of the Conquest of New Spain, 1632) almost fifty years later at the age of seventy-two. He portrays the Spanish soldiers as the collective heroes of the conquest. His detailed, dramatic account of the soldiers, battles and landscape makes his history one of the most important chronicles written about the conquest from the Spanish point of view.

Besides the Mayan texts and Díaz del Castillo's chronicle, important writers did not emerge in Guatemala until toward the end of the nineteenth century. This can be explained, in part, by the long colonial period under Spain's domination and the strong, although at times ineffectual, censorship that the mother country exercised. The Spanish Inquisition severely curtailed freedom of expression. Would-be writers were loathe to risk facing the fearsome inquisitors if a work was deemed heretical.

RAFAEL GARCÍA GOYENA

One important exception was a neoclassic writer of fables, Rafael García Goyena (1766–1823), who is claimed as a national writer by both Ecuador, where he was born, and by Guatemala, where he spent most of his life. He became recognized throughout Latin America for his fables, which were short, allegorical pieces that depicted animal characters. They were typical of neoclassic, didactic tendencies that were meant to impart the difference between right and wrong according to the moral tenets of the time.

ENRIQUE GÓMEZ CARRILLO

Although there were other writers during the Colonial period, the next recognized Guatemalan writers appeared during the period of *modernismo* (Latin American modernism). Although deeply influenced by European tendencies, this is considered the first true Latin American literary movement. *Modernista* writers, principally poets, were primarily concerned with developing the aesthetic nature of literary language. *Modernismo* became associated with elegant, sophisticated, musical and select verbal expression, frequently evoking exotic, aristocratic worlds replete with plastic imagery. Although it has been labeled escapist poetry, especially in its later stages, *modernismo* achieved profound depths. It represented human anguish and disillusion in the face of an increasingly indifferent, materialist society. It also addressed encroaching U.S. imperialism. Enrique Gómez Carrillo (1873–1927) became one of the most important *modernista* writers of Guatemala. He was influenced by the great Nicaraguan poet Rubén Darío and by other precursors of *modernismo*, such as the Cuban patriot and writer José Martí. Gómez Carrillo was recognized throughout Latin America for his considerable work as a journalist, critic, novelist and chronicler. He was appointed consul to Argentina, wrote extensively for Spanish and Latin American journals and traveled throughout the world. His vivid, perceptive, original descriptions of the landscape, cities, books and individuals he encountered in his travels earned him the title of "the creator of the modern chronicle." He published numerous collections of chronicles, including the following: *El alma encantadora de París* (The Enchanting Soul of Paris, 1902); *De Marsella a Tokio y Desfile de visiones* (From Marseilles to Tokyo, and Parade of Visions, 1906); *El Japón heroico y galante* (Heroic and Gallant Japan, 1912); *La sonrisa de la esfinge (Egipto)* (The Smile of the Sphinx, 1903); *El encanto de Buenos Aires* (The Enchantment of Buenos Aires, 1914); *La Rusia actual* and *La Grecia eterna* (Russia Today and Eternal Greece, 1920).

In Paris, he became friends with numerous famous Spanish and French intellectuals and with other Latin American authors residing there, such as Rubén Darío. Bohemian by nature, his scandalous love life and his reputation for speaking his mind almost eclipsed his reputation as a writer. One may say that although Gómez Carrillo played hard, he also worked hard. Proof of this is that his completed works consist of twenty-seven volumes of chronicles, criticism, novels and recollections. His writings reflect both his vast knowledge of literature and the private life of famous writers and intellectuals whom he came to know quite well in Europe.

Gómez Carrillo's prose reflected the *modernista* tendencies of the time. His style is musical, colorful and elegant, demonstrating his preoccupation with a pure, aesthetic language. Although he also wrote novels in the *modernista* style, they did not achieve the artistic reputation of his chronicles, nor of his autobiography that was published in three volumes and is entitled *Treinta años de mi vida* (Thirty Years of My Life, 1920–1923).

RAFAEL ARÉVALO MARTÍNEZ

The other foremost Guatemalan *modernista* and post-*modernista* writer is Rafael Arévalo Martínez (1884–1975), who came of age during the peak of *modernismo* but whose form and content rapidly evolved into a different, original, creative, imaginative mode. He was born in Guatemala City to parents of humble origins, and he grew up working at various odd jobs until he received his bachelor's degree. In 1912 he became the chief editor of the newspaper *La República*. He also was a professor in various schools and universities in Guatemala. He was the director of the National Library from 1926 to 1946 and served as ambassador to the Organization of American States from 1945 to 1946.

Arévalo Martínez became one of Guatemala's foremost writers, distinguishing himself as a poet, short-story writer, dramatist and essayist. Although his first poems, which appeared in his book *Maya* (1911), were heavily influenced by Darío's early ornamental style, his poetry matured into a simpler, less-adorned form in *Los atormentados* (The Tormented Ones, 1914), *Las rosas de Engaddi* (The Roses of Engaddi, 1918), *Llama* (Flame, 1934) and *Por un caminito así* (Along that Little Pathway, 1947). However, Arévalo Martínez is known mostly for his prose, especially for introducing a style in the Latin American short story that he called "psycho-zoological." In these stories the characters take on human and animal attributes, combining them in such a way to stress the analogies between their physical and psychological traits. In *El hombre que parecía un caballo* (The Man Who Looked Like a Horse, 1915), the similarities of the life of a Columbian poet, Porfirio Barbra Jacob, to a horse are underscored. Through the use of interior monologue the story becomes a penetrating psychological study of the inner consciousness of the character. In other stories the protagonists are compared to animals to the point that one may say that Arévalo Martínez practically creates a zoo. *El trovador colombiano* (The Colombian Troubadour, 1914) portrays a hero who combines the characteristics of a human and a dog. In *El señor Monitot* (Mr. Monitot, 1922) the protagonist is seen as an elephant. The dove, the snake, the tiger, the bull and various birds of prey also appear in the story. In several stories, Latin American dictators are portrayed as animals. The worlds that Arévalo Martínez depicts are fantastic creations of his imagination, combined with psychological insights into the human character and the subconscious.

Arévalo Martínez's autobiographical novels include *Una vida* (A Life, 1914), *Manuel Aldano* (1914) and *Las nochas en el palacio de la nunciatura* (Nights in the Palace of the Nunciature, 1927). Among his sociopolitical novels are *La oficina de paz de Orolandia* (The Peace Office of Orolandia, 1925), which depicts U.S. imperialism in Central America, *Viaje a Ipanda* (Voyage to Ipanda, 1939) and *El mundo de los maharachías* (The World of Special Creatures, 1939). This last novel is a fantastic vision of a universe that is inhabited by bizarre creatures who combine human and animal characteristics and have long, magnificent tails that are sensitive organs.

GENERATIONS OF 1920 AND 1930

In the first half of the twentieth century a group of left-wing writers emerged in Guatemala who became identified as the Generations of 1920 and 1930. These writers suffered censorship and violent repercussions under the dictatorship of Estrada Cabrera and Jorge Ubico. Many of them fled into exile only to return with the triumph of the revolutionary governments of Juan José Arévalo and Jacobo Arbenz Guzmán. During this period various literary groups found freedom to express their ideological views. Among them was the Marxist-oriented Saker-ti (meaning "dawn" in Mayan). Created in 1947, it included such writers as Miguel Angel Vásquez, Carlos Illescas, Raúl Leiva, Olga Martínez Torres, Melvin René Barahona and Augusto Monterroso (Zimmerman, 1995). However, at the end of the Ten Years of Spring, and with the return of a series of dictatorships, most of them were forced to leave the country once more. These writers were quite aware of the deep cultural divisions in their country between the Ladinos and the majority Mayan population. This preoccupation, apparent in their writings, attempted to address what they called "*el problema del indio*" ("the Indian question"). Although they should be applauded for drawing attention to a submerged and disguised question of national identity, their approach tended to be assimilationist and integrationist, basically advocating the Ladinoization of the Mayas, which implied an end to their cultural identity. Four important writers of this period were Luis Cardoza y Aragón, Mario Monteforte Toledo, Miguel Angel Asturias and Augusto Monterroso.

LUIS CARDOZA Y ARAGÓN

Luis Cardoza y Aragón (1904–1992) was born in Antigua, Guatemala, and grew up under the shadow of Guatemalan dictators Estrada Cabrera and Ubico, a time when it was very difficult to develop artistically without fear of censorship. He was exiled while still an adolescent because he directed a weekly opposition journal. He traveled to Paris in 1921, where he met important Latin American writers such as Enrique Gómez Carrillo, Alfonso Reyes, César Vallejo and Alejo Carpentier. He also met André Bretón and other important surrealists. Influenced by them, in 1924 at the age of nineteen he published *Luna Park*. In 1927 he published *Maelstrom: Films telescopiados* (Telescopic Films). These books of experimental poetry earned Cardoza his early reputation as a Latin American vanguard poet. Cardoza traveled to Cuba and New York. He arrived in Mexico in 1932, where he lived for twelve years, and became part of the League of Revolutionary Writers and Artists. He became friends with the great Mexican muralist Diego Rivera. Cardoza became an art critic, writing important critical essays on Mexican paintings in his books *La nube y el reloj* (The Cloud and the Watch, 1940) and *Apolo y Coatlicue*. He continued to write poetry. Through the years he published poetic works such as *Pequeña sinfonía del Nuevo Mundo* (Small Symphony of the New World, 1948), *El sonámbulo* (The Sleepwalker, 1937), *Dibujos de ciego* (Blind Drawings, 1969), the anthology *Quinta estación* (Fifth Season, 1972), and a collection of his works, *Poesías completas y algunas prosas* (Complete Poems and Some Prose, 1977).

Cardoza returned to Guatemala to become part of the revolutionary spirit that swept the country with the governments of Juan José Arévalo and Jacobo Arbenz Guzmán. He founded the important *Revista de Guatemala* (Guatemalan Journal), and worked as a diplomat for the revolutionary governments, serving as ambassador to the Soviet Union. Upon returning, he founded the Casa de Cultura (House of Culture).

When the military dictatorship was reestablished in 1954, Cardoza returned to exile in Mexico, where he published his masterpiece, *Guatemala, las líneas de su mano* (Guatemala, the Lines of Your Hand, 1953). This is a profound narrative written in prose and poetry that analyzes Guatemalan history and literature. Angry and nostalgic, this Guatemalan epic reflects on the country's political and social realities. It delves into the psychological effects of a brutal history that has muzzled the people and forbidden them from developing their creativity or escaping an all-pervasive sadness that dominates Guatemalan culture. He states that "nuestro silencio está hecho de canciones que no hemos podido cantar" (our silence is composed of songs that we have not been able to sing) (Cardoza y Aragón, 1953). The indigenous population has an important place in the essay, and Cardoza contrasts the view of the colorful, picturesque Maya of the highlands with the pain and suffering of a population silenced by hundreds of years of oppression. Although at times he stereotypes the Mayas, Cardoza's work prods a new awareness of the situation of the Maya in Guatemalan history and culture.

MARIO MONTEFORTE TOLEDO

For many years Mario Monteforte Toledo's works remained in obscurity due, in large part, to the silence that the dictatorships imposed after the 1954 coup. As a consequence of a fanatical anticommunist stance, the military dictatorships censored any work that even remotely suggested a criticism of the government or sympathy for the previous leftist administrations of Juan José Arévalo and Jacobo Arbenz Guzmán. Monteforte's works were banned and were read only clandestinely in university classrooms. Also, because he was viewed as an *indigenista* writer (a writer of indigenous themes) during a time when *indigenismo* (literature focusing on indigenous themes) was viewed with some skepticism, his works did not receive widespread attention until the mid-1970s, when popular movements of resistance again focused on "the Indian question" and a new interest in *indigenista* literature was revived (Liano, 1984).

Monteforte left Guatemala in 1931 after he was ejected from the University of San Carlos for his opposition to Ubico's dictatorship. He traveled to Paris where he came into contact with the surrealist movement, as had many other Latin American writers, including his compatriots Asturias and Cardoza y Aragón. He returned to Guatemala in 1937 and moved to the Mayan area of Sololá, where he gained firsthand knowledge of Mayan culture and traditions. As a nascent sociologist, he used his observations and experiences of everyday life in the Indian towns of Nahualá and San Pedro la Laguna as a basis for his *indigenista* works, escaping from the picturesque tradition of *indigenismo* to a social-realist stance. What he portrayed, however, was filtered through his Ladino point of view, and it is permeated by certain stereotypical depictions and a paternalistic attitude toward the Indians.

His most important work is *Entre la piedra y la cruz* (In Between the Stone and the Cross, 1948). It describes the problems of Indian and Ladino workers on a coffee plantation owned by Germans. It focuses on the dilemma of a young Maya, Luz Matzar, who is torn between a desire to integrate himself into Ladino society or to maintain his Mayan culture. In the end he joins the Ladino revolutionary struggle and marries a Ladina woman, signifying his assimilation into Ladino culture and a separation from his Mayan identity. This assimilationist view was a central aspect of Monteforte's ideology and is especially considered problematic today, particularly by Mayan intellectuals.

Monteforte served as Juan José Arévalo's vice president in the 1940s. He left in 1951 because of his disagreement with the direction of the socialist government. He continued writing novels, essays and sociological treatises.

Some of his other works include the following: *Guatemala. Monografía sociológica* (Guatemala. Sociological Monograph, 1959), a long, sociological discourse on the geographic, demographic, historic, political, economic and social factors that have formed Guatemalan realities; *Donde acaban los caminos* (Where the Paths End, 1953), the story of a Ladina doctor who abandons his Indian lover to marry a rich Ladina; *Una Manera de morir* (One Way to Die, 1957), which focuses on the difficult years of alienation and exile following the U.S. intervention and overthrow of Arbenz Guzmán in 1954; and *Y llegaron del mar* (And They Arrived from the Sea, 1966), which advocated the integration of Mayas into the dominant Ladino culture. Despite Monteforte's paternalistic attitude toward the Indians and sexist depictions of sexual acts and gender relations, his works constitute an important chapter in Guatemalan literary history.

MIGUEL ANGEL ASTURIAS

Guatemalan literature of resistance to the dictatorships of Estrada Cabrera and Ubico reached its culmination with *El señor presidente* (Mr. President, 1946), Miguel Angel Asturias' (1899–1974) masterpiece novel about dictatorship for which, largely, he received the Nobel Prize for literature in 1967. Although Asturias wrote the novel during the 1930s, he had to wait until after the 1944 revolution to publish it because of its chilling depiction of an unspeakably sadistic, corrupt and omnipresent dictator who still ruled Guatemala in the form of Ubico during the 1930s. The plot is complex and interwoven with numerous subplots; seemingly unrelated characters appear and disappear, forming a myriad of grotesque, greedy, cowardly and weak individuals, which is the legacy of a society accustomed to being dominated by terror. The few courageous individuals who rebel are imprisoned, brutally tortured, mutilated and murdered. Space becomes a claustrophobic, dark, suffocating horror, either in the prisons where many of the characters meet their end, or in domestic spaces that are also dominated by terror. Although not named, the nation itself is seen as a prison from which there is no escape because the president knows and sees all. The narrator, who is omnipresent like the president, does not reveal everything to the reader, who must decipher the psychological dimensions of the characters as they interact in their social milieu. Although mostly recognized as a portrayal of a vicious dictatorship, *El señor presidente* is also an aesthetic, original and poetic creation of language. The power of the narrative imagination is reflected in an onomatopoeic, melodious language that is abundant with metaphors, neologisms, regionalisms and oral vulgarities, the last verbalized by the slum dwellers, street urchins, prostitutes and some of the other crass characters. This rich poetic language transforms some of the harshest elements into another reality; hence the interplay between conscious reality and the subconscious that is revealed in dreams and nightmares, streams of consciousness, fantasies, memories, sensations and a mythological world. The interaction between light and dark imagery reflects the forces of good and evil, life and death, linking space and time to an infernal world that a terrifying dictatorship controls. At the novel's end the ruthless president has brutally crushed any perceived opposition, including that of his former favorite, Miguel Cara de Angel (Angel Face), who goes mad while rotting in a tiny, black, fetid hole of a dungeon.

On a metaphysical level, the main plot may be perceived as the struggle between life and death. Miguel Cara de Angel, the president's former henchman, falls in love with the daughter of a renegade general who the president seeks to destroy. Love transforms him and operates as a vital force that opposes the president's power of death, ultimately converting Miguel into the president's enemy. Because Miguel is inside the system and is a trusted ally of the president, the betrayal is perceived as far worse than that of outside resistance. The final confrontation between the two becomes an enactment of Mayan Quiché mythology, with the president seen as Tohil, the rain god who demands human sacrifice, and Miguel Cara de Angel as the hunters about to be sacrificed. Since the latter symbolize fertility, the encounter is between life and death forces. And because Miguel Cara de Angel leaves a son behind who is the product of the love that redeemed him, life forces triumph over the president's evil, homicidal plan (Callan, 1970).

El señor presidente is a novel that is mostly about Ladino urban life under a dictatorship. The country of reference could be any Latin American nation, although there are some cultural elements, such as language and Mayan mythology, that identifies it as Guatemala. The indigenous element appears more prominently in Asturias' other works, at first with negative connotations. Asturias was aware of the division in his society between Indians and non-Indians, and he attempted to address it through a mostly assimilationist approach. His dissertation, which he completed in 1923, was an analysis of "The Social Problem of the Indian," a stereotypical depiction of the Mayas that advocated the improvement of their race by crossbreeding it with superior European races and assimilating it into the dominant Ladino culture. Implicitly this means the eradication of Mayan culture, a thesis for which Asturias was and is harshly criticized by Mayan intellectuals and other advocates of indigenous cultural autonomy.

Asturias' later works demonstrated that his perspective had matured and evolved into one that recognized the importance of Mayan culture. He lived in Europe for ten years and the influence of the French surrealists becomes apparent in his first book, *Leyendas de Guatemala* (Legends of Guatemala, 1930), which also integrates elements of the *Popol Vuh*. He returned to Guatemala in 1933, which was still under the yoke of dictator Jorge Ubico. Under the revolutionary government of Juan José Arévalo, Asturias became the Guatemalan cultural ambassador to Mexico in 1945. It was there that he published *El señor presidente*. He also served as cultural attache to Argentina.

In 1949 he published his other masterpiece, *Hombres de maíz* (Men of Maize). This complex, seemingly disorganized novel is almost incoherent for most readers, but it is rich in Mayan cosmogony, myths and history. It is held together by an underlying narrative thread that is based on Mayan and Aztec mythology that connects the different sections. The title is taken from the Mayan story of creation, related in the *Popol Vuh*, in which the gods struggle to find the right element to create humankind. After various failed attempts, they finally settle on maize, from which they mold humans. (Hence the importance of corn as a source of physical and spiritual nourishment to the Mayas.) The novel depicts the struggle of the Mayas to preserve their culture. It is laden with Mayan myths, legends, and magical visions that give it a unique dreamlike quality, reflecting various ethnic and mythical interpretations of daily and epic phenomena.

In 1950 Asturias published *Viento fuerte* (Strong Wind, or The Cyclone), the first book of his banana trilogy, which describes the repercussions of the presence of the United Fruit Company in Guatemala. When President Jacobo Arbenz Guzmán was overthrown in 1954, his successor, dictator Carlos Castillo Armas, stripped Asturias of his Guatemalan citizenship. Asturias left to live in exile for the next five years in South America. During that time he published the second and third novel of his banana trilogy, *El papa verde* (The Green Pope, 1954), and *Los ojos de los enterrados* (The Eyes of the Interred, 1960). He also published *El alhajadito* (The Bejeweled Boy, 1961), and *Mulata de tal* (The Hybrid Mulata, 1963). The latter is based on a popular Mayan Quiché folktale about the consequences that a man pays for selling his wife to the devil. Asturias also published a travel book on Romania, various plays, poetry and essays. He was awarded the Lenin Peace Prize in 1966, and he was named ambassador to France that same year. In 1967 he became the second Latin American writer (after the Chilean Gabriela Mistral) to receive the Nobel Prize for literature.

Augusto "Tito" Monterroso

Also writing in the 1950s and 1960s while living in exile in Mexico was Augusto "Tito" Monterroso (1921–). He was born in Honduras of a Guatemalan father and a Honduran mother. He moved to Guatemala as a child, where he lived until 1944, when he went into exile in Mexico. Because he has lived in Mexico since then, both Guatemala and Mexico claim him as one of their writers. However he considers himself Guatemalan. As with other Central American writers, Monterroso's work has not received the kind of critical acclaim that it deserves.

Before he went into exile in 1944, Monterroso was active in the political movements that opposed the dictator Jorge Ubico. Monterroso was one of 311 people who signed a petition demanding his resignation. After he lost his job for provoking a strike, and after Ubico's successor, Ponce Vaides, censored Monterroso's opposition newspaper, *El Espectador*, Monterroso went into exile. But during the terms of Presidents Arévalo and Arbenz Guzmán, the brief Ten Years of Spring, Monterroso served as Guatemalan vice counsel to Mexico and then as counsel to Bolivia. He quit his diplomatic post when Arbenz Guzmán was overthrown in 1954. He then spent two years in exile in Chile, where he became good friends with the famous Chilean poet Pablo Neruda. He later returned to Mexico and became a professor at the Universidad Autónoma de Mexico, where he established his reputation as a writer of the short story and the literary essay.

Although he participated actively in protest marches and other actions in Guatemala against Ubico's dictatorship, Monterroso states that he has never viewed literature as a political instrument. He does, however, admit that many of his stories address social dilemmas, which may be why some readers deem his stories political. A master at brevity (one of his stories consists of one sentence), his stories are intricately structured, highly ironic pieces that play with society's perceptions of present and past realities. "El eclipse" (The Eclipse), one of his first published pieces, appeared in the newspaper *El Siglo* in Chile while he was living there. It was published in his book *Obras completas y otros cuentos* (Complete Works and Other Stories, 1959). It has been seen as a response to the then popular Tintin comic books that the Belgian Hergé created in which Latin Americans are portrayed as lazy, witless, naive savages incapable of governing themselves without European help (Binns, 1997). In Monterroso's story the knowledgeable, wise Indians triumph over European ethnocentric superiority.

One of Monterroso's most popular short stories, the first to appear in his *Obras completas*, is "Mr. Taylor." In this story the stereotypes of Latin Americans as seen from a U.S. perspective are portrayed in a highly ironic and farcical manner. The protagonist from the United States, Mr. Taylor, becomes involved in the shrunken-head business to such an absurd extent that it causes the self-extermination of entire tribes of Indians and eventually leads to the shrunken head of Mr. Taylor himself. The story may be read both as a commentary on the dangers of U.S. imperialism for Latin American cultures and as a critique of old colonial practices of exploitation that eventually return to haunt the colonial powers.

Ten years after the *Obras completas*, when he was just about forgotten, Monterroso published *La oveja negra y demás fábulas* (The Black Sheep and Other Fables, 1969). These fables, quite distinct from traditional ones, are ironic, humorous pieces that depict animal characters, famous personalities and classical writers. The stories represent the futility and vanity of human undertakings. The fables are notorious for their endings, which invert accepted societal notions and go against the lessons of so-called common sense. *Movimiento perpetuo* (Perpetual Motion, 1972) is a hybrid book of different genres, including short stories, essays, prose poems and pages from his memoirs. *Lo demás es silencio* (The Rest Is Silence, 1978) is a novel about a mediocre, fictional Mexican writer, Eduardo Torres. It is about writers in general and presents an ironic, autobiographical depiction of Monterroso himself. Monterroso has also published *Viaje al centro de la fábula*. (Journey to the Center of the Fable, 1981) which is a book based on interviews between the author and other writers, allowing Monterroso to expound his ideas on writing and literature. His other works include an autobiographical essay entitled *La letra "e": Fragmento de un diario* (The Letter "E": A Fragment of a Diary, 1987) and a short memoir, *Los buscadores de oro* (The Gold Seekers, 1993).

MANUEL GALICH, OTTO RENÉ CASTILLO

Manuel Galich and Otto René Castillo were also resistance writers. Galich, in *Del pànico al ataque* (From Panic to Attack, 1949), wrote an important testimony based on his own reflections about the urban rebellion against the dictator Ubico in the 1930s and 1940s.

Castillo was part of a group of Central American writers who called themselves "La generación comprometida" (the Committed Generation). Castillo was eighteen years old when the CIA-sponsored coup overthrew President Jacobo Arbenz Guzmán in 1954. Like other Guatemalan revolutionaries, Castillo went into exile in El Salvador, where he was active in revolutionary activities and became known as a poet. He returned to Guatemala in 1957 and continued his revolutionary activities there by becoming a part of university life and founding the dissident journal *Lanzas y letras* (Lances and Letters). He became involved in a movement of documentary filmmaking, which was led by Dutch director Joris Ivens, that sought to depict revolutionary struggles throughout Latin America. In 1965 he published a book of poetry, *Vámonos patria a caminar* (Let Us Move Forward, Nation), that revealed his commitment to armed struggle. At various times Castillo suffered repercussions because of his political activities. This is evident in both his life and his works. He actively worked with the guerrillas, believing that the commitment of the intellectual had to match that of the active revolutionary. Unlike many of his Marxist comrades, he also understood the importance of the participation of the Indians in the revolutionary conflict and the need to study their cultural realities. While fighting with his guerrilla comrades against the military in 1967, he was captured, brutally tortured and burnt alive. Castillo became a symbol of the Central American poet-revolutionary, the committed intellectual who gave his life for the ideals about which he wrote.

LUIS DE LIÓN DÍAZ AND OTHER WRITERS OF THE 1970S

The years of harsh repression after 1954 took their toll on writers, who became increasingly fearful of expressing their views. Writers ideologically opposed to the dictatorships that ruled their country had to find more innovative, indirect linguistic means to express their discontent. An example of this technical experimentation is Luis de Lión's *El tiempo principia en Xibalbá* (Time Begins in Xibalbá), which was written in the early 1970s but not published until 1985. In this novel of no characters and no plot the narrative voice is mixed with that of the Mayas of an unidentified village, becoming a collective of voices that underscore the oral nature of Mayan culture (Arias, 1995). Luis de Lión was born in Sacatepéquez in the Mayan highlands in 1939. His indigenous roots are evident in his depiction of the Mayan world, which he portrays from an erotic, if at times *machista* (male-centered), perspective. His protest against Mayan oppression by the Ladinos resulted in his "disappearance" in the early 1980s.

In the late 1980s and early 1990s, Central American writers in general lost faith in the ability of literature to create a class consciousness or to imagine national projects of social transformation (Arias, 1995). As a result of the defeat of the Sandinistas in Nicaragua and the end of the guerrilla insurgencies in El Salvador and Guatemala, writers concentrated on a transformation at a linguistic level rather than on the traditional, realistic form.

Instead of depicting brutal government or military oppression directly, it is represented through innovative linguistic and formal techniques in allegories. *Los compañeros* (The Comrades, 1976) by Marco Antonio Flores is generally regarded as the first novel of a new narrative style in Guatemala. The stylistic innovations, the criticisms of the failed guerrilla movement and the condemnations of government and military violence all broke with past traditions and anticipated the testimonial novel (Zimmerman, 1995). Marco Antonio Flores, Arturo Arias, Mario Roberto Morales, and Edwin Cifuentes formed part of a group of writers in the 1970s who deviated from traditional fiction forms and created a new narrative style that dealt with similar issues but experimented with different styles and structures. There is no identifiable authoritarian narrator and no main character. Time and space are ruptured, and the narrative engages a variety of voices at different levels, frequently through interior monologue or stream-of-consciousness techniques. The texts challenge the perceptions and understandings of the readers and force them to unravel the symbolic dimensions of Guatemalan history and culture.

At the same time that the new novel was emerging, testimonial narratives became increasingly important in Guatemalan literature. But they worked at a symbolic, collective level rather than as a personal, individual history (Arias, 1995). These works represent real experiences but in a fictionalized, artistically elaborated style. This is distinguished from traditional *testimonios*, in which the predominant concern to denounce the historic conditions of brutality and oppression takes precedence over artistic intricacies. Examples of this style are Mario Roberto Morales' *Señores bajo los árboles* (Men Under the Trees, 1994) and Arturo Arias' *Después de las bombas* (After the Bombs, 1979). Employing stream of consciousness and monologues that continue after the death of the subject, Morales' novel portrays the scorched-earth policies of the Guatemalan military dictatorships, which razed entire indigenous villages and practiced genocide against the Mayas in the late 1970s and 1980s. The novel depicts the Mayas as caught between the guerrillas and the military, preferring to have nothing to do with either. The book represents a collective protest against their oppression (Craft, 1997).

ARTURO ARIAS

Arias' obsession with the history of Guatemala is tied to his own personal experiences in Guatemala after 1954, which in turn are connected to the culture of the young Guatemalan bourgeoisie (Liano, 1984). The title of his first novel, *Después de las bombas* (After the Bombs, 1979), refers to the CIA-inspired coup in 1954, when the revolutionary government of Jacobo Arbenz

Guzmán was overthrown and replaced by a series of military dictatorships. The text is the story of a young protagonist who grows up in the midst of the repression and is witness and victim to Guatemala's bloody and painful history of the period, losing his father to the violence. Arias uses the popular language of the Guatemalan bourgeois youth, but he does so in a highly ironic manner to caricature certain well-known political figures or locations, distorting terms to the point of achieving a grotesque dimension. Historic events are represented allegorically as absurd deformations that are closer to the truth than "official" history. For example, an arm wrestle decides a presidential election, and suspected Communist sympathizers are publicly executed to cheering, brainwashed crowds. In the end the protagonist, in exile, achieves a level of consciousness that induces him to become part of the struggle against the oppression of his people. But he does this through writing rather than through violent means. The power of words is underscored in the protagonist's decisions to bring his father back to life through writing and to represent the struggle of his people. Through his irreverent and satiric portrayal of Guatemalan history, Arias invites the readers to engage with his text and come up with their own conclusion.

Arias' second novel, *Itzam-ná* (1981), named for a Mayan god, won the prestigious Casa de las Américas (House of the Americas) prize. In a highly sarcastic, humorous and grotesque manner, Arias portrays the bloody period of Guatemalan history between 1978 and 1988 in which over 100,000 people, mostly Mayas, were massacred and a million people displaced. The characters are indulged youths from the upper classes who rebel against the traditional values of their parents by adopting the hippie modes that are popular in the United States, such as smoking marijuana and experimenting with LSD. The novel portrays the disorientation and contradictions of these youths as they search for their roots in a confused interpretation of a Mayan cosmovision. Their self-destructive actions anticipate the demise of the egotistic, rapacious, dominant class.

Arias' other novels are *Jaguar en llamas*, (Jaguar in Flames, 1989) and *Los caminos de Paxil* (The Paths of Paxil, 1990). Like his previous works these books juxtapose contemporary Guatemalan society and history with a Mayan submerged past that emerges through the use of myth, magic and other Mayan cultural beliefs and practices.

RIN-78

During the 1970s a short-story writer and literary promoter, Max Araujo, founded a group of writers from various political persuasions who worked together to find ways to publish their works and those of others under the extremely repressive regime of Lucas García. The group included important writers and critics such as Dante Liano, Luz Méndez de la Vega, Hugo Estrada, Mario Alberto Carrera, Francisco Alizúrez Palma, Carmen Matute, and Luis Enrique Sam Colop. The group, entitled RIN-78, was instrumental in finding ways for certain urban Guatemalan writers to produce and publish their works (Zimmerman, 1995).

RIGOBERTA MENCHÚ

In 1976 Gabriel García Márquez, the Colombian Nobel laureate, referred to the repression in Guatemala as worse than elsewhere in Latin America. He said that this was not so much because of its long history, the intense ferocity and the lack of compassion amongst the perpetuators, but rather because no one remembered or cared about it (Arias, 1995). The events of the late 1970s and 1980s, however, propelled Guatemala back into memory and into the international arena, especially with the publication in 1983 of the famous and highly controversial *testimonio* of a Quiché Mayan activist, Rigoberta Menchú.

The traditional *testimonio* concerns itself less with artistic expression and more with revealing conditions of suffering and oppression among the marginalized classes. It is not meant to be a blueprint of reality, but rather it acts as a prism through which reality is filtered due to the fluctuations of memories of the subjects who relate their testimonies. Although there were many other important *testimonios* in Central America before the Menchú's, the genre came to the fore in Latin America with her testimony, which focused attention on the plight of the Mayas, who were systematically undergoing a process of extermination in their own country. Twenty-three-year-old Menchú was visiting Paris as a representative of Frente Popular 31 de enero (Popular Front January 31, an organization whose name commemorates the anniversary of the massacre of her father, Vicente Menchú, and 30 peasant supporters) that was fighting government oppression at the time. There she met Venezuelan-French ethnographer Elisabeth Burgos and agreed to a series of interviews that lasted eight days. Burgos recorded, transcribed and edited the *testimonio*. Because Menchú was not yet adept at the Spanish language, Burgos corrected grammatical errors and organized the narrative into thematic sections to make it a coherent narrative.

In her *testimonio*, *Me llamo Rigoberta Menchú* (I, Rigoberta Menchú), Menchú described the customs and practices of her Mayan community, which have been passed down through a rich oral tradition from generation to generation. The importance of nature and ancestral connections, and the intimate relationship between the land and the Mayas, are portrayed in a vivid, lyrical prose that emphasizes the importance of a harmonious, reciprocal correlation between nature and humankind. Also described are the discrimination and brutal repression that the Mayas suffered at the hands of the Ladinos. This is first described as part of daily life and then as a full-scale holocaust when the military dictatorships under generals Lucas García and Efraín Ríos Montt imposed their scorched-earth policies to eradicate the guerilla insurgency in the highlands. The military was allowed to raze entire Mayan villages, indiscriminately torturing, mutilating, raping and murdering the residents to eliminate any population from which the guerillas could possibly receive supplies or support. The government bragged about its success at burning down 440 Mayan villages (although the number documented by the Historical Clarification Commission in February 1999 was closer to 626). Tens of thousands of Indian civilians were massacred and a million more displaced, many of them fleeing into Mexico. Among the victims were Rigoberta Menchú's brother, mother and father. Their tortured deaths and those of others are anguished portrayals of her people's pain in the face of brutal policies of extermination. Menchú also had to flee for her life.

From its very inception Menchú's testimony was surrounded by controversy. This started at a moral and formal level (what constitutes "truth" and what constitutes "literature") and then became a direct, personal attack on Menchú's character. The attacks were intensified after she won the 1992 Nobel Peace Prize, a symbolic recognition and commemoration of the marginalized indigenous peoples of the Americas.

Dinesh D'Souza's *Illiberal Education*, which celebrated traditional canonical works and disparaged marginal literatures, dedicates an entire chapter to Menchú's testimony, which is scornfully entitled "Traveling with Rigoberta." D'Souza's contempt for Menchú, her testimony and her culture is apparent in numerous disparaging remarks, such as his description of Menchú's wearing of her "tribal garb," rather than Western clothing. And yet he gets almost everything wrong about Menchú and her testimony (such as placing Guatemala in South America), and serves as an example of why the traditional, narrow academic focus that he advocates should be widened to include marginalized writings to better educate a misinformed public about the global community in which they live.

After D'Souza there were other attacks on Menchú and Burgos' text, culminating in the assault by U.S. anthropologist David Stoll, who spent years of his life probing into the veracity of Menchú's testimony about the genocide of her people. Although Stoll's assertions had been known for a long time, at least since 1991 when they were debated at the Latin American Studies Association meetings, they gained international attention at the end of 1998 when his account was published on the front page of the *New York Times*. To corroborate Stoll's claims, the *New York Times* sent an investigative reporter to Guatemala and found that there were discrepancies in Menchú's testimony. For instance, her brother was not burnt to death as described in Menchú's testimony, although others from her community were, but rather killed by a firing squad and thrown into a mass grave. Another revelation was that her father was not involved in a struggle for land with the elite landowners, but rather he was in a dispute with Mayan relatives. Although this may not have been Stoll's purpose, by pinpointing certain variances in Menchú's text, the *New York Times* article had the effect of dismissing the account of the genocide of tens of thousands of Mayas, among whom Menchú's family members figure. Nobody disputes that her father, peasant organizer Vicente Menchú, was burnt alive in the Spanish embassy in Guatemala City with thirty other civilian protesters, or that her mother was raped, tortured and mutilated before being murdered by the military, or that she lost two brothers to the violence. Whether or not one of Menchú's brothers died in the manner described in her text would hardly seem to matter as the Mayas bury their dead. Also, that Menchú's father was involved in a struggle with relatives over parcels of land is indicative of the scarcity of land available for the Mayas. Unable to challenge those in power, who are backed by government and military might, they must bicker among themselves for the paltry leftovers of a colonial legacy over 500 years old.

That Rigoberta Menchú's testimony may convey partiality does not detract from the urgency of the overall message. Ironically, that message is undermined by turning the victim into the guilty party. This is especially tragic at a time when the violence and repression continues despite the signing of the peace accords in Guatemala. The signing had the effect of virtually erasing the country from the international map again because peace has theoretically been achieved and all is supposed to be well. Western intellectuals seem to be more interested in attacking Menchú than in disseminating information about the continued brutality against her people. One must question these choices. Menchú describes her point of view and dilemmas in her book *Rigoberta: La nieta de los mayas* (Crossing Borders, 1998).

Menchú's testimony does not stand in isolation. There are also accounts from groups that monitor human rights, such as Americas Watch and Amnesty International, and the thousands of testimonies put together by Bishop Gerardi before he was assassinated in 1998, others by the Jesuit Ricardo Fallas in his collective testimony, *Masacres de la selva* (Massacres in the Jungle,

1992), and the guerrilla testimony of Mario Payeras, *Días de la selva* (Days of the Jungle, 1980). Also, Mayas other than Menchú have produced testimonies about their experiences and the suffering of their people. Among these indigenous testimonies, one may perceive a certain trend that moves from a Mayan oral tradition, reflected in the oral nature of Menchú's testimony, to a written form, apparent in the testimony of the Maya Victor Montejo and in the testimonial novels of Q'anjobal Mayan writer Gaspar Pedro González.

VICTOR MONTEJO

Victor Montejo's *Testimony: Death of a Guatemalan Village* (1987) was first published in English. Guatemalan writer Victor Perera translated it after Montejo fled to the United States to live in exile. A Spanish edition, *Testimonio: Muerte de una comunidad indígena en Guatemala*, was not published until 1993. Montejo's educated status is underscored by his profession as a schoolteacher in a highland Mayan village; hence his ability to write rather than dictate his testimony. In his narrative Montejo describes the sleepy, anonymous village where he taught between 1980 and 1982, which fell victim to the government's policy of establishing "civil patrols," vigilante groups that were required to report to the military any suspicious activities among the villagers. In Montejo's testimony an army unit disguised in guerrilla fatigues is mistaken for actual guerrillas and attacked by the village's "civil patrol." The rest of the testimony is a wrenching, haunting, painfully vivid description of the psychological abuse and physical torture of the townspeople, who are accused of being in league with the guerrillas. The brutal execution of innocent, frightened villagers and the coercing of villagers to kill each other or be killed are described in graphic, chilling detail. Montejo, as schoolmaster and the most educated person in the town, assumed a leadership role in attempting to convince the military that the attack was an accident. He paid the price by being subjected to imprisonment and torture. He was also forced to observe the most gruesome forms of human punishment imaginable. The testimony ends with the flight of Montejo and his family into exile. Since then Montejo has published other works, such as *The Bird Who Cleaned the World* (1991), a book that retells Mayan folktales, and *Las aventuras de Mister Puttison entre los mayas* (The Adventures of Mister Puttison among the Mayas, 1998), a satirical, often humorous, often painful portrayal of U.S. anthropologists who travel to Guatemala to study the Mayas.

GASPAR PEDRO GONZÁLEZ

Gaspar Pedro González's first testimonial novel, *La otra cara* (A Mayan Life, 1992), was originally written in his native language of Q'anjobal. González rewrote it in Spanish. It was later translated into English and numerous other languages. The author does not attempt to directly reproduce the experiences or voices of witnesses as other testimonies discussed here do. He was a witness to the events that he narrates, which represent the situation of countless Mayas living in the highlands. In this sense, the fictionalized protagonist, Luín, represents a collectivity. The oral nature of *La otra cara* is illustrated by the abundance of dialogues, the reproduction of sounds in written form and the narrative blank spaces that represent pauses. Rich Mayan cultural traditions are described in the novel, such as rites involving birth, courtship, marriage, folklore and myth.

The story is a *bildungsroman* (coming-of-age tale) of the young Luín, who is obliged to attend a Ladino school, the only school in the area, to learn how to read and write. Run by a Ladina teacher and dominated by Ladino students, Luín rapidly learns that he is considered inferior. He suffers discriminatory treatment and physical abuse by the teacher and her Ladino students. The few isolated Mayan students internalize their experiences and come to believe that they really are ethnically or racially inferior to the Ladinos. This leads to the eventual Ladinoization of those Mayas who become ashamed of their ethnicity and attempt to pass as non-Indians. Luín himself goes through a process of self-doubt, but as he matures he begins a series of conversations with others in his community about the alleged Maya inferiority. They conclude that their inability to perform well in school is not because of an innate inferiority, but rather it is due to the economic, political and social circumstances in which they live. These circumstances include the lack of electricity, the scarcity of educational materials, the lack of potable water, the prevalence of disease and sickness due to malnutrition, the hostility in a Ladino environment, the arduous and time-consuming tasks that must be performed to help parents, and the conditions of harsh poverty in which the majority of the Mayas live. This analysis of Luín and his community represents the introspective nature of González's work in an exploration of the historic reasons that have led to the inequitable living conditions of the Mayas at the end of the twentieth century.

González's second novel, *El retorno de los mayas* (The Return of the Maya, 1998) is also focalized through the point of view of a young Mayan boy, this time one who flees for his life with his mother and sister after his father is assassinated and his village is razed. It is a painful account that attains biblical proportions. It describes the exodus of thousands of persecuted Mayas as they perish in the jungles while attempting to reach the border of Mexico. The Mayas find the strength to continue from the practices of their ancestors and their intimate connection with their natural gods. The title refers to the return of Mayan refugees to Guatemala, which was negotiated during the signing of the 1996 peace accords, in the hope that they would be allowed to live in peace.

During the fifteen years from Menchú's published testimony in 1983 to this second testimonial of González in 1998, there was a certain evolution toward a more introspective analysis of how the Mayas view themselves and toward how they believe the Ladinos view them. A long oral tradition, which is now being reproduced in written form by the Mayas themselves, offers another vision of history that serves as an opening for other literary works. This creates a dialogue in which, finally, they themselves can participate. This progression is evident in that the most famous testimony was not written but dictated by Menchú, while González's first testimonial novel, *La otra cara*, was not only written by a Maya but may be considered the first modern Mayan novel. These texts represent an effort to reclaim the past of the Mayas, to analyze their present, and to look to the future, offering a wider lens through which to view the history that hundreds of thousands of Mayas live.

HUMBERTO AK'ABAL

An important Guatemalan poet, a man who gained international prestige in the late 1980s and early 1990s and has been translated into numerous languages, is the Maya Humberto Ak'abal. Born in the town of Momostenango, in the heart of Quiché in 1952, Ak'abal decided to become a poet at a young age despite economic obstacles. He developed his talents first in his native Quiché language, later translating his poems into Spanish. In his poetry Ak'abal portrays the visual and auditive beauty of nature, which is filtered through a uniquely Mayan perspective that seems to capture the essence of animals, plants, bodies of water, light, darkness and other everyday encounters with nature. At times this is reflected in erotic longings for the soul mate. In his oral recitations, Ak'abal has enchanted his public with his close imitations of bird songs and other animal sounds. His poetry also speaks to the sorrow of the poverty and oppression that the Mayas have endured throughout the centuries. Two of his collections of poetry are *El animalero* (The Animaler, 1991) and *Guardián de la caída de Agua* (The Guardian of the Falling Water, 1991).

CONTEMPORARY WOMEN WRITERS OF GUATEMALA

Women writers in Guatemala followed the widespread historic trend in Latin America of generally limiting themselves to writing poetry, as the writing of novels was considered unfeminine and the domain of men. These poets were women from the middle and upper classes who had received some form of education and were able to pursue their vocations in private and/or under pseudonyms during the Colonial period and the nineteenth century. With some exceptions they wrote about traditional themes of family life, religious inspiration and romantic love. Anticipating the emergence of feminist writing in the later twentieth century, some wrote about the dissatisfaction of women who were trapped in a *machista* (male-oriented), double-standard society that limited their choices and curtailed their sexual and creative freedom.

During the 1970s and 1980s there was a flourishing of women's poetry in Guatemala, much of it from a feminist, political perspective that was mostly from a privileged, non-Indian point of view. The most famous exception is Rigoberta Menchú, who began publishing her testimonial poetry, in which the Mayas are the collective subject, in the 1990s.

An earlier example is Caly Domitila Cane'k, a catechist and teacher, who wrote poetry in the 1980s in her native Kaqchikel language that described the destruction of her town and people during the state-sponsored massacres of the late 1970s and 1980s. After several of her brothers were assassinated in the northern part of highland Guatemala where she lived, Cane'k was forced to flee into exile. Her poem in Kaqichikel, "They Destroyed My Mother's House," has been translated into Spanish and English. It is a moving account of the grief and suffering of her parents and her community in the face of the violence. Its tone is similar to that of Gaspar Pedro González in *El retorno de los mayas*.

Luz Méndez de la Vega published refined poetry with political and feminist content in the 1970s. Méndez is a journalist and briefly directed the cultural supplement of *La Hora*. Her poetry mourns the shadow of death that permeates different sectors of Guatemalan society under the rule of oppressive regimes. It also satirizes the racist and sexist dimensions of patriarchal domination in such feminist works as *Eva sin Dios* (Eve Without God, 1979) and *Las voces silenciadas: Poemas feministas* (The Silenced Voices: Feminist Poetry, 1985). Overtly political poetry emerged with Julia Esquivel Velázques. In *El padre nuestro desde Guatemala y otros poemas* (Our Father from Guatemala and Other Poems, 1981), she condemns the oppression and bloodshed of the Mayas and the Ladino poor. She also has a bilingual edition of her poetry, *The Certainty of Spring* (1993). Other feminist poetry emerged with such writers as Carmen Matute, Marta Mena, Isabel de los Angeles Ruano, Delia Quiñónez, Margarita Carrera, Alaíde Foppa and especially Ana María Rodas. Foppa lived in Mexico for many years after the 1954 coup with her husband Alfonso Solórzano, a Guatemalan politician. During this period of exile she became active in feminist activities, especially the Guatemalan women's movement. Two of her volumes of poetry are *Elogio de mi cuerpo* (Eulogy to My Body, 1970) and *Las palabras y el tiempo* (Words and Time, 1979). Upon returning to Guatemala she was kidnapped and murdered by the death squads, becoming a martyr and a symbol of Guatemalan women's resistance.

Ana María Rodas

Ana María Rodas, a journalist, literary critic and professor, became known and celebrated mostly for her book of poetry *Poemas de la izquierda erótica* (Poems of the Erotic Left, 1973). In the poem that coined the term "erotic left," Rodas satirizes a system in which men who use violence to transform societies, such as the revolutiary Che Guevara, become heroes whose image is disseminated through popular culture on posters, T-shirts, banners, and so on, while women who struggle to change society through love and words, "guerrillas of love," go largely unnoticed. Rodas condemns the oppressive regimes that dominate her country, but she is also critical of the *machismo* prevalent in left-wing intellectuals. She reveals the hypocrisy of the leftist revolutionary who publicly calls for equality and justice for all, but in his home rules over women just like the tyrants he condemns. Among her other books of poetry are *Cuatro esquinas del juego de una muñeca* (Four Corners in the Doll Set, 1980), *El fin de los mitos y los sueños* (The End of Myths and Dreams, 1984) and *La insurrección de Mariana* (The Insurrection of Mariana, 1993). She won the first prize in the Certamen de Juegos Florales Mexico, Centroamerica y el Caribe (Literary Contest of Floral Games, Mexico, Central America, and the Caribbean) in 1990.

Isabel Garma

Norma García Mainieri was an important woman fiction writer of the 1980s. While living in Mexico she published her collection of short stories, *Cuentos de muerte y resurrección* (Stories of Death and Resurrection, 1987), under the pseudonym Isabel Garma. Her stories vividly depict the dark era of bloodshed in Guatemala. The stories often have realistic details and at other times are tinged with surrealism. "El pueblo de los seres taciturnos" (The Village of the Taciturn People), is a story about the massacre of an entire village. The populace of the neighboring town, many of whose relatives and friends lived in the eradicated village, go through a process of voluntary memory loss to avoid confrontation both with the truth and with the military authorities who are responsible for the massacre. It is a dramatic metaphor for the loss of memory and identity that the dispossessed, who experience violent trauma and have no means of redressing the tragedy of their people, often suffer.

GUATEMALAN AMERICAN WRITERS

Two important Guatemalan American writers are Victor Perera (1934–) and Francisco Goldman (1955–). Perera translated Victor Montejo's *Testimony: Death of a Guatemalan Village* (1987) into English in 1987. In *Rites* (1986) and *The Cross and the Pear Tree* (1995) he explores what it is like to be Jewish in Latin America (Craft, 1997). Goldman's novel, *The Long Night of the White Chickens* (1992) is woven in a maze of intrigue that involves an illegal adoption ring making millions through the sale of babies to foreigners. Although the plot takes place in an unidentified nation, the descriptions of places and people, the role of the military and the references to the Indian holocaust place the action in Guatemala. It is a fascinating, bittersweet exploration of the psychological workings of Ladino urban society.

CONCLUSION

With its roots in pre-Columbian Mayan texts and the subsequent influence of the Europeans, Guatemalan literature has passed through phases that reflect the historic, political and cultural conditions of certain periods. At the end of the twentieth century a new generation of Mayan authors is emerging that heralds a new age of Mayan literature. Many Guatemalan writers, influenced by Western models, have experimented with avant-garde literary techniques that reflect unique Mayan-Ladino motifs. More Guatemalan women writers are also emerging as a significant cultural and literary presence. Guatemalan literature is gaining increasing international attention. Today it stands at the brink of new discovery, an unfolding of immense creative potential. As Guatemala comes to terms with its rich, divided cultural heritage, its centuries-old literary tradition promises to continue in an even more fertile vein in the third millennium.

REFERENCES

Anglesey, Zoe. *Ixok Amar-Go: Central American Women's Poetry for Peace.* Penobscot, ME: Granite Press, 1987.

Arévalo, Teresa. *Rafael Arévalo Martínez: Biografía de 1926 hasta su muerte en 1975* (Biography from 1926 Until His Death in 1975). Guatemala City: Oscar de León Palacios, 1995.

Arias, Arturo. "Conciencia de la palabra: Algunos rasgos de la nueva narrativa centroamericana." *Hispamérica: Revista de literatura* 61 (April 1992): 41–58.

———. "Descolonizando el conocimiento, reformulando la textualidad: Repensando el papel de la narrativa centroamericana." *Revista de crítica literaria latinoamericana* 21.42 (1995): 73–86.

———. *Gestos ceremoniales.* Guatemala City: Artemis-Edinter, 1998.

Barcárcel, José Luis. "Literatura y liberación nacional en Guatemala." *Casa de las Américas* 126 (May–June 1981): 17–26.

Barrientos, Alfonso E. *Enrique Gómez Carrillo.* Guatemala City: Editorial José Pineda Ibarra, 1973.

Bellini, Giuseppe. *La narrativa de Miguel Angel Asturias.* Buenos Aires: Losada, 1969.

Beverley, John. "The Real Thing." In Georg M. Gugelberger, ed., *The Real Thing: Testimonial Discourse and Latin America.* Durham, NC: Duke University Press, 1996.

Beverley, John, and Marc Zimmerman. *Literature and Politics in the Central American Revolutions.* Austin: University of Texas Press, 1990.

Binns, Niall. "Tintin en Hispanoamérica: Augusto Monterroso y los estereotipos del cómic." *Cuadernos Hispanoamericanos* 568 (October 1997): 51–66.

Bogantes, Claudio, and Ursula Kuhlmann. "El surgimiento del realismo social en Centroamérica, 1930–1970." *Revista de crítica literaria latinoamericana* 9.17 (1983): 39–64.

Callan, Richard. *Miguel Angel Asturias.* Boston: Twayne, 1970.

Cardoza y Aragón, Luis. *Guatemala, los lineas de su mano* (Guatemala, the Lines of Your Hand). México, D.F.: Fondo de Cultura Económica, 1953.

Craft, Linda. *Novels of Testimony and Resistance from Central America.* Gainesville: University Press of Florida, 1997.

D'Souza, Dinesh. *Illiberal Education: The Politics of Race and Sex on Campus.* New York: Free Press, 1991.

Fischer, Edward F., and R. Mckenna Brown. *Maya Cultural Activism in Guatemala.* Austin: University of Texas Press, 1996.

Garcia Escobar, Carlos Rene. "Los actuales tiempos y los escritores." *La Hora,* September 12, 1992, *Cultural.*

Giron Mena, Manuel Antonio. *Rafael Arévalo Martinez: Su vida y obra.* Guatemala City: Editorial José de Piñeda Ibarra, 1974.

Krauel, Ricardo. "La república clausurada: análisis de los espacios opresivos en *El señor presidente.*" *Monograhic Review/Revista Monografica,* 11 (1995): 220–34.

Liano, Dante. *La palabra y el sueño.* Rome: Bulzoni Editore, 1984.

Masoliver, Juan Antonio. "Augusto Monterroso o la tradición subversiva." *Cuadernos Hispanoamericanos* 408 (1984): 146–54.

Mendoza, Juan Manuel. *Enrique Gómez Carrillo: estudio crítico-biográfico: su vida, su obra, su época.* Guatemala City: Tipografía Nacional, 1946.

Noguerol Jiménez, Francisca. "Textos como 'esquiralas': Los híbridos genéricos de Augusto Monterroso." *Insula* 618–619 (June–July 1998): 29–32.

Nyrop, Richard T., ed. *Guatemala: A Country Study.* Washington, DC: The American University of Washington, Foreign Area Studies, 1983.

Prieto, René. *Miguel Angel Asturias' Archaeology of Return.* Cambridge: Cambridge University Press, 1993.

Stavans, Ilan. "On Brevity: A Conversation with Augusto Monterroso." *Massachusetts Review* 37.3 (1996): 393–403.

Stoll, David. *Rigoberta Menchú and the Story of All Poor Guatemalans.* Boulder, CO: Westview Press, 1999.

Tedlock, Dennis, trans. *Popol Vuh.* New York: Simon & Schuster, 1985.

Zimmerman, Marc. *Literature and Resistance in Guatemala.* Athens: Ohio University Press, 1995.

———. "Testimonios in Guatemala: Payeras, Rigoberta, and Beyond." *Latin American Perspectives* 18 (Fall 1991): 22–47.

7

Performing Arts

THE PERFORMING ARTS in Guatemala are a reflection of the ethnic and cultural mix of its Mayan, Ladino and Garífuna populations. In the Guatemalan highlands, for example, there exists of a rich tradition of dance-dramas that are central features in most local festivities. These dances reflect hundreds of years of the coexistence of Mayan and Christian beliefs. They stem from pre-Columbian times and represent the clash of cultures and the subsequent historical developments. In the cities, dance is a more traditional affair, modeling itself after European masters. At the beginning of the century theatrical productions were largely representations of European pieces, such as Spanish Golden Age dramas, but eventually they evolved to reflect Guatemalan social realities. Contemporary theater was especially stimulated during the years of the Arévalo and Arbenz Guzmán presidencies (1944–1954), during which various dramatists experimented with new techniques. In recent years efforts have been undertaken to make theater more accessible to the general public.

Music also reflects the diverse nature of Guatemala's population. The National Symphony Orchestra of Guatemala is one of the best orchestras in Latin America. Guatemalan rock groups have been heavily influenced by international trends, and they continue to develop along original and revolutionary lines. The Guatemalan marimba is popular throughout the country and is rarely absent from major, official celebrations. Garífuna musicians of Livingston play traditional instruments of African origin along with modern instruments that lend the music a unique rhythm.

TRADITIONAL DANCES OF GUATEMALA

In Spanish there are two different terms that refer to dance: *danza* and *baile*. Although at times the terms overlap, *danza* refers to ritualized, choreographed and rehearsed dances with indigenous elements. *Baile* is used for informal, spontaneous or couple dancing, more along the Western model. The dances described here can be characterized as *danzas*, although some of them have also been called *bailes*. Perhaps the best way to describe *danzas* in this context is as dance-dramas.

Many dances in Guatemala, as in Latin America in general, have their origins in the dances and rituals that the pre-Columbian civilizations of Spain and America practiced. With the clash of cultures that evolved after 1492, most dances became a blend that reflected certain traditions, cultures, and histories of Europe and America. Predominant, however, was the religious element. Besides the accumulation of the riches for personal use and for the Spanish Crown, the driving force behind the Spanish conquest of America was the evangelization of the Indians. The central purpose of missionaries who accompanied the Spanish conquistadors was to save the souls of those whom they considered to be pagan—and therefore damned—Indians. After the initial brutality of the invasion and as the missionaries became acquainted with the customs and traditions of the Indians, many of them allowed the Indians to continue to practice their cultural activities but with a Christian slant. Because the Indians had a different form of written expression and did not initially understand alphabetic writing, the missionaries rapidly learned that they were most successful in imparting their messages in visual and oral forms. They introduced certain Spanish art forms, such as the *teatro misionero* (missionary theater) that they found attracted and impressed the Indians with the Christian message in a way that straightforward lectures, threats and punishments did not. The missionaries were most successful in converting the Indians from their native religions to Christianity through these syncretic cultural practices, many of which continue in varying forms today. In Guatemala, as elsewhere in Latin America, many cultural practices have their roots in a blend of Catholic and native rituals that have passed through centuries of variations and local interpretations, reflecting the historic, political and cultural manifestations of the moment.

Dance in Guatemala is one of the syncretic practices that has evolved at a local level to become a popular feature of most religious and national festivities. It is rare to celebrate an occasion without some form of dance, especially in the indigenous towns and villages. Many of these festivals are in honor of a patron saint. They can last two days or more and involve music, dance, drink, and food. Throughout generations the dances have evolved to reflect the customs, language and taste of the locale. It is unusual to see the same dance practiced in exactly the same manner in different villages. However, the central theme of a dance may be common in diverse and distanced locations, reflecting the pre-Columbian origins that have traversed through time.

It is particularly clear that the dances in the highland, indigenous communities of Guatemala reflect the religious blend that stemmed from the end of the fifteenth and the beginning of the sixteenth century. Other dances reflecting the African influence of the Garífuna or Garínagu are practiced in the northeast region of Guatemala and in Belize and northern Honduras. A popular dance that emerged at the end of the nineteenth century was the *son*, which takes on its own ethnic, cultural and local color depending on whether it is danced by the Mayas or the non-Indians, The *son* and popular music became diffused throughout the country through the use of mass communication, especially radio (García Escobar, 1996). In fact, it is unusual to ride a public bus without some kind of popular music blasting from the bus radio.

One of the popular dances performed today throughout Guatemala that exemplifies the above discussion is *El Baile de los Moros y Cristianos* (The Dance of the Moors and Christians). It is part of festivities in the central and western highlands, on the southern coast, in northern Alta Verapaz and in the east in Chiquimula. There are numerous variations of this dance. But the historical context emerges from the year 711, when the Moors conquered Spain. They cohabitated with the Spanish until 1492, when the Spanish Reconquest was completed and the Moors were driven out of Spain. It was during the sixteenth and the seventeenth centuries that the heroes of the Spanish conquest became the subject of legends that were inscribed in manuscripts, song and dance. However, it is believed that *El Baile de los Moros y Cristianos* was performed in Spain as early as the twelfth century. In these expressions the Christian Spaniard always triumphed over the pagan Moor. When the dance was introduced in the American context, it became a battle between good and evil, or Christians versus the pagans. The New World was a particularly fertile ground for this kind of dance performance, and the missionaries used it to dramatize the conflict between God and the devil. They allowed the Indians to add their own cultural twist to make it a combination of Christian and indigenous practices.

Although there are numerous variations, generally there are thirteen male dancers. They represent six Christians, six Moors and one Moorish princess (played by a male). The storyline of one version, "El Español" (The Spaniard), is that the Spanish King, Don Fernando de Castilla, is angry because King Botargel of the Moors has stolen a crown that the Spanish king kept in his temple to crown the Virgin Mary of the Conception. But the Moorish king wished to crown his daughter, who lived in Rome, with the stolen crown. The situation rapidly deteriorates into one of warfare in which each king is supported by five warriors. In the battle the Christians capture king Botargel, who is saved by his princess daughter. She offers to convert to Christianity and convinces her father to do so if King Fernando spares their lives. King Fernando does so. The Moors convert to Christianity. And the crown is returned to the Virgin for whom it was intended (García Escobar, 1990).

Besides the male dancers, participants involve the women who prepare food and drink. Participants must pay their dues and attend the rehearsals. Young male dancers, usually children, are initiated by playing the role of the Moorish princess. Others who establish reputations as talented dancers or as respected members of the community gradually assume the role of the Christian or Moorish kings. They wear colorful costumes with elaborate masks, and other props, such as swords or crowns, that identify them as Moors or Christians. Generally, the occasion for the dance is a religious one, celebrating the triumph of Christianity over paganism. Local musicians playing popular instruments, such as the drum and whistle, accompany the dance. All participants memorize their roles. The dancers recite their lines as they dance, although it is difficult to hear them through their masks. The dance itself is formatted as a contradance, with two armies facing each other and waging war. Generally, the spectacle lasts about two hours.

Besides "El Español," the dance has other names in different areas, such as "Carlo Magno" (Charlemagne), "La Conversión de San Pablo" (The Conversion of Saint Paul), "La Reina Catalina" (Queen Catherine), "El Rey David" (King David), "Granada" and many others. There are also a variety of other dances that have their roots in a mix of pre-Columbian and Spanish traditions. It is believed that *El Baile de los Gigantes* (The Dance of the Giants), for example, has its roots in the Mayan-Quiché creation epic, the *Popol Vuh*, and in European and biblical tales of mythological giants. The biblical tale of David and Goliath became the subject of a dance during medieval times in Europe, and today a version is practiced in Honduras ("Baile-drama de David y el Gigante Goliat"). Other legendary European giants were Hercules, Atlas, Gargantúa and Anteo. Although it is not certain, it appears that *El Baile de los Gigantes* arrived with the Spaniards in Guatemala around the end of the seventeenth century. It then acquired its own ethnic variation as the Indians interpreted it according to their beliefs, some of which are reflected in the *Popol Vuh*. In the *Popol Vuh*, before the creation of humankind, giants played ball with the mountains, and they made the mountains and the valleys tremble as they walked through them. These giants were eventually defeated by the hero twins Hunahpú and Ixbalanqué (García Escobar, 1987).

Stories about the giants are very popular in local communities. According to legends the giants existed in the countryside in the past, and at times they came to town to dance. Since they died, the townspeople built their own symbolic *gigantes* (giants) to remember them. The structures are generally owned by a *cofradía* or by local elderly inhabitants who lend them out or rent them during festivals. The giants, two females and two males, are built of wood more than two meters high. They are covered by yards of cloth, usually floral, and equipped with arms and heads that are generally sculpted from wood. Two of the heads are customarily painted white and two are painted black, although the reasons for this are not clear. Perhaps they represent the same battle between good and evil as in *El Baile de los Moros y Cristianos*. When it is time to dance, the men enter the wooden structures and dance to marimba music, bending over to scare and thrill the spectators (García Escobar, 1987).

Another popular dance that is practiced in Mexico, Nicaragua and Guatemala is *La Danza del Palo Volador* (The Dance of the Flying Post). Records of this dance exist in the writings of the first Spanish chroniclers. The roots of the dance are in the famous chapter of the *Popol Vuh* in which the 400 boy-heroes are killed by Zipacná, the giant mover of mountains. Today the dance is practiced in Chichicastenango, Joyabaj, Quiché, Cubuclo and Baja Verapaz. The villagers must select a giant tree to be the post from the which the dancers fly. Twenty to hundreds of men help to strip the 30 to 40 meter tree and carry the post to the center of the town plaza, where they bury the tree two meters into the ground. A small, rotating, basketlike platform is erected at the top where the thick cables are attached. In one version there are four "flyers" in bird or monkey costumes. Another eight "Moors and Christians" dance on the ground. Two of the "flyers" go to the top platform and facilitate the rotation of the basket. The other two fly around and around the post, suspended vertically by their knees attached to the cables, heads downward and arms outstretched, as they simulate the act of flying. The dancers take turns flying until all of them have had the opportunity. As they descend they embrace and thank the tree for not allowing any mishaps. It is a dramatic, and ancient ritual that certain men of the village perform (women are excluded), accompanied by prayer and incantations to ward off bad spirits and influences. It is also accompanied by marimba music, which apparently was an element that was added after the arrival of the Europeans. Taking the post down and either saving it for another festival or chopping it up for wood for the dancers is also an important part of the ritual (García Escobar, 1970).

There are many other dancers that mostly Indian groups in the highlands practice. In these dances one perceives the blend of Mayan creation myths and history with biblical traditions and Spanish folklore and history. The dancers combine the Mayan central concern of death with the Spanish pre-occupation with salvation (Edmonson, 1997). The rite of sacrifice plays a meaningful role in many of the dramas. An important pre-Columbian dance-drama is the *Rabinal Achi* (people of the town of Rabinal), which has been translated from Quiché into numerous languages. It tells the story of a Qui-ché prince who is captured and executed by the warriors of the prince of Rabinal. Other popular dances are the *Baile de la Conquista (Dance of the Conquest)*, which reenacts both the initial contact between the Spaniards and the Mayans and the confrontation between the Spanish conquistador Pedro de Alvarado and the Mayan warrior Tecún Uman. The *Baile de Toritos* (Dance of the Bulls) mimics the Spanish bullfight.

The Guatemalan anthropologist Carlos René García Escobar, who has minutely studied these traditional dances, categorizes them into various groups involving myths, hunting, warriors, pastoral themes, agrarian themes, livestock, diversions, and ethics, some of which overlap into other categories. Although these dances have disappeared in some areas of the country, the numerous ones still performed during Christian holidays and the days of the patron saints of the scattered towns in the highlands indicate that they are a popular tradition with deep roots in indigenous and Christian belief systems. That thirty dance-dramas have been performed multiple times in the Quiché area alone during the twentieth century, while twelve others date to colonial times, reflects their ritual and cultural importance (Edmonson, 1997).

There is a difference between these traditional rehearsed dances and those spontaneously executed, which are called *bailes*, during all kinds of festivities. Some examples are the *sones*, the *vals*, the *danzón*, the fox trot and the *gua-rimba*. These are mostly practiced by the non-Indian population (García Escobar, 1989).

BALLET

Guatemala has the only professional ballet company in Central America. Called El Ballet de Guatemala, it has thirty Guatemalan dancers. They have performed dozens of classical works, such as *Don Quijote* and *Giselle*, and original Guatemalan compositions such as *Roots* and *Ixquic*. Brought to Guatemala in 1948 by a Belgian couple, Jean Devauz and Marcelle Bonge, a ballet teacher and ballerina respectively, the company has been very successful and has performed internationally throughout Central America, the United States, Germany, and in other Latin American countries. At a local level it has numerous fans who attend the diverse functions. At times it is intended for serious ballet audiences, and at times it caters to young children (Darer, 1998).

MUSIC

Garífuna Music of Guatemala

The Africans began to arrive in the Americas on Spanish ships early in the sixteenth century. The famous Spanish conquistador Hernán Cortés brought along a group of Africans on his voyage to Honduras (Beltrán, 1984). The records kept under the governorship of the founder of Spanish Guatemala, Pedro de Alvarado, demonstrates that there was already a significant population of Africans present in Guatemala at that time. With the increase of the African slave trade in subsequent years, this population grew to form an important cultural component of Guatemala. In the early 1700s escaped or shipwrecked African slaves began to arrive on the islands of the Antilles, especially in San Vicente. The indigenous Carib-Arawaks initially did not welcome them. But in the face of their common enemy, the White man, they eventually formed alliances and intermixed. From this miscegenation the Garífuna were born. They are descendants of the Africans and Arawaks. They speak the native Arawak language sprinkled with African terms.

After much warfare, at the end of the eighteenth century the English gained control over the Garífuna and deported them to the Islas de la Bahía, off the coast of Honduras. From there the Garífuna spread to certain areas of what became Belize and Nicaragua. In present-day Guatemala they form the majority population of Livingston and Puerto Barrios in Izabal, between Honduras and Belize. They speak their own Garífuna language, worship their ancestors, practice oral literature, have their own traditional social organizations based on family and brotherhoods, and ritualize their particular history, such as the arrival of the first Garífuna to this region.

Music is one of the most important aspects of Garífuna culture, and most Garífuna grow up playing instruments. Children at a very young age learn to make music out of discarded household items, such as pots, pans, spoons and matchboxes. *Combos infantiles* (groups of children) form groups to make music together. Different kinds of music are associated with various activities, such as songs in honor of the ancestors, songs for Christian rituals organized by the churches, songs for collective work projects and songs for processional bands. This last category is composed of musicians playing trumpets, trombones, clarinets, saxophones, drums and cymbals, who play during feasts or ritual occasions such as Holy Week. During these times they play funeral or other religious music in processions to mourn the passing of Jesus Christ. It is said that Livingston bands used to play fox trot, ragtime, blues and music to accompany square dances in the city's plaza. But this is no longer true.

There are numerous ways in which people express themselves musically. The *combos infantiles* are composed of young people who play drums, jingles, trumpets, clavichords, electric guitars or keyboards. They play traditional rhythms during festive occasions. There are groups dedicated to studying the musical tradition among the Garífuna to ensure its preservation and continuity. There is also the mass-produced music that is distributed on cassettes, records and CDs or played over television and radio, where one can hear merengue, calypso, soca and reggae. The most traditional Garífuna music is played on drums called the garaon, which is accompanied by jingles. A choir sings and dances to mimic what the lyrics express. The African influence is apparent in the predominance of an oral tradition (Arrivillaga Cortés, 1990).

The Guatemalan Marimba

The marimba, a kind of wooden xylophone, has become closely identified with Guatemalan culture and national identity. Many believe that the marimba originated among the Mayas before the Spaniards arrived. The marimba, like the quetzal bird, has become a national symbol of pride for Guatemala, symbolizing the independent nature and originality of Guatemalan culture. It has also become a source of contention because the Guatemalan roots of the instrument have been challenged. Various musicologists, among them the renowned Cuban scholar Fernando Ortiz, have claimed an African origin for the instrument, believing that it arrived in Cuba and certain areas of Guatemala with the African slaves. Others believe that it originated in Asia. And others find ample evidence to show that it is a product of acculturation among the Mayas, Spaniards and, some believe, Africans. The marimba, then, appears to be a *mestizo* instrument (Monsanto, 1982). As such it has certain characteristics in Guatemala that differentiate it from marimbas played elsewhere in the world. However, nationalists argue vehemently against any of these opinions insisting that the marimba is strictly Guatemalan.

A controversy arose in Guatemala in 1976 when a monument to the marimba was to be erected in Quetzaltenango. A poem honoring the marimba was to be engraved on the monument, and the choice of that poem inflamed political passions on the Right and Left, also involving Ladinos and Mayas. The source of contention was the differing opinions of the origin of the marimba. There were those who insisted that it was a native instrument and therefore a source of nationalist pride and those who were called "traitors" because they believed otherwise (Monsanto, 1982). The monument was finally dedicated in 1978. The controversy demonstrated not only the importance of the marimba as a national and cultural symbol, but also revealed the political tensions that were dominating Guatemala at that time.

The Cuban ethno-musicologist Fernando Ortiz believes that the marimba is so widely popular in Central America and Mexico because the Indians there played a similar instrument called the tun, teponaztli, or teponaguaste, a wooden drum that combined elements of the xylophone. Eventually, the Mayas adopted the European scale, and European melodies became popular. Mixing these with native rhythms produced a popular dance, the *son chapín* (Guatemalan son) (Monsanto, 1982).

The earliest written reference to the marimba is from the inauguration of a cathedral in 1680 in the old capital of Guatemala (now Antigua) (Juarros, 1937). Today the Mayas primarily make and play the marimbas on numerous festive occasions in cities and villages throughout Guatemala. In fact, it is rare to have a feast without marimba music. Constructing a marimba, sometimes described as a wooden piano, so that it produces a refined, melodious tone is a challenging artistic construct for the local artisans. *Marimbistas* play music from all over the world, including pieces by Beethoven, Mozart, Bach, de Falla and Villa-Lobos. Some famous Guatemalan *marimbistas* are the brothers Hurtado, the brothers Ovalle, Salomón Argueta and Fernando Morales Matos.

The Symphony

The National Symphony Orchestra of Guatemala was born in 1941 in the years immediately preceding the revolutionary government of Juan José Arévalo. Formerly known as the Progressive Orchestra, it was renamed to bring it under the purview of the Ministry of Communications and Public Works, thereby making it a government-sponsored cultural entity.

The symphony's first season was in 1946. Directors of symphonies from other countries participated. This trend has continued and contributes to making it one of the top symphonies in Latin America. Currently the symphony is directed by Nestor Arévalo, who began to study music at the age of twelve at the National Conservatory. He studied violin under the renowned Carlos Ciudad Real. He later studied in the United States and France. In 1991 the musicians of the symphony were successful in reaching an agreement to establish their own board of directors. Besides being the concert master, Nestor Arévalo now is president of that board.

The National Symphony Orchestra of Guatemala plays in schools and universities during the months of April, May and June. The official season begins July 30 and continues through November. The concerts are held at the National Theater every other Thursday evening and feature famous classical composers.

Rock

Guatemalan rock music arrived in the 1980s with Alux Nahual ("Spirit of the Goblin," in the Quiché language). They have been pioneers in revolutionizing the music scene in Guatemala and Central America with their unique style, which is a combination of classic-rock music and native music. They use traditional rock instruments (electric guitar, drums, bass, keyboard) and nontraditional ones (cello, dulcimer, saxophone, harmonica, acoustic guitar, water rod). Alux Nahual was the first large-scale concert band in Central America. Before them public performances were mostly spectacles put on by popular dance troupes, and rock music was dominated by foreign groups.

The local and international success of Alux Nahual opened the door to other Guatemalan rock groups, who have flourished in the 1990s. Many of them began their careers at the popular Bodeguita del Centro, an informal performance space in downtown Guatemala City. Some of the most notable are Bohemia Suburbana, Domestic Fool, Extinción, Fábulas, La Tona, Viento en Contra, Viernes Verde, Malacates Trébol Shop and Radio Viejo.

CONTEMPORARY THEATER

The Teatro Colón (Colón Theater) in Guatemala City was the center of the theatrical activities from its inauguration in 1859 until the massive earthquake of 1917 destroyed the building. During those years the main theatrical activities centered on operas and *zarzuelas* (Spanish musical comedies) that were performed by foreign theater companies. In 1909 a smaller theater, Teatro Variedades (Theater of Variety) opened. In both theaters Spanish Golden Age plays were frequently performed. In 1917 the Teatro Colón, the Teatro Variedades, and a smaller theater, Teatro Abril, were all seriously damaged by the earthquake, leading to the eventual demolition of the Teatro Colón in 1922. Meanwhile the Grupo Artístico Nacional (Artistic National Group) began performing open-air theater. They later found a place to perform in the newly erected El Renacimiento Theater (Renaissance Theater) across the street from the Teatro Colón. This group at first performed foreign plays, but it gradually began to put on local dramas, thus initiating a national theater.

In the 1920s the state began to contribute a small amount of money toward the production of plays. This and the reopening of the Teatro Variedades and, eventually, the Teatro Abril helped motivate local interest in the theater. However, the world depression of 1929 that caused drastic economic problems in Guatemala dried up any resources that were intended for theater. And under the dictatorship of Jorge Ubico, theater was severely curtailed, because foreign theatrical companies were not permitted in Guatemala. In 1935, when the economic crisis was under control, theater was granted a certain amount of freedom. The state sponsored some cultural activities to honor both the centennial anniversary of the birth of Guatemalan dictator Justo Rufino Barrios and the tricentennial anniversary of the death of the famous Spanish playwright Lope de Vega. Guatemalan dramatists such as Manuel Galich and María Luisa Aragón were encouraged to produce works that were performed mostly by the Grupo Artístico Nacional. This tendency to at least tolerate the production of dramas, as long as they remained apolitical, lasted until 1944.

Under the presidency of Juan José Arévalo, theater received new life in 1945, especially through his appointment of María Solá de Sellares as the director of the Instituto Normal para Señoritas Belén (Belén Normal Institute for Young Women), which would train many of the successful actors and actresses of subsequent decades. At first only women participated, even playing the roles of male characters. However, by 1947 male students from the Universidad de San Carlos began to participate, which led to the creation of the Teatro de Arte Universitario (Theater of University Art) in 1952. Under the direction of Carlos Mencos, this theater would continue to operate until 1980.

The female students from the Belén Institute who went on to become important elements of Guatemalan theater included the following: Norma Padilla, actress and head of the Directorship of the Theater Department of Culture and Fine Arts for almost twenty years; Matilde Montoya, actress and researcher of indigenous colonial theater; Ligia Bernal, actress, writer and head of the Department of Aesthetic Education; Carmen Antillón, promoter of puppet theater; and Consuelo Miranda, actress, director and teacher. Although most plays put on at the time were foreign, some began to explore local myths and legends. And Guatemalan dramatist Manuel Galich began to gain importance with the performance of two plays, *Ida y Vuelta* (Round Trip, 1950), and *La Mugre* (Greasy Dirt, 1953), both put on by the short-lived Teatro de Arte Guatemalteco (Theater of Guatemalan Art, 1950–1953).

With the violent overthrow of President Jacobo Arbenz Guzmán in 1954, the small financial contributions from the state for theater that were managed by the minister of education were relocated to the secretary for the popularization of tourism. The principal focus became the production of large-scale events that would attract tourism, particularly the Festival of Antigua Guatemala, which was first held in 1956.

The years between 1945 and 1959 established a base for future Guatemalan theater. In the 1960s the most important group that came into being was the Compañía de Arte Dramático de la Universidad Popular (Company of Dramatic Art of the Popular University). Under the direction of Rubén Morales Monroy, the group dedicated itself principally to performing Guatemalan dramas, especially in the yearly Festival de Teatro Guatemalteco (Festival of Guatemalan Theater), which began in 1962. Important performances were *La piedra y el pozo* (The Stone and the Pit) by Ligia Bernal, *El profeta* (The Prophet) and *Orestes* by Manuel José Acre, and *La calle del sexo verde* (The Street of the Green Sex) by Hugo Carrillo. The last two were quite controversial for their political and sexual themes. There were also presentations of *El tren amarillo* (The Yellow Train) by Manuel Galich and *La audiencia de los confines* (The Audience of the Borders) by Miguel Angel Asturias. Other important Guatemalan dramatists were Carlos Solórzano, Victor Hugo Cruz, María del Carmen Escobar, María Luisa Aragón, Ernesto Mérida, Augusto Medina, Carlos Menkos, Adolfo Drago Braco, Miguel Marisicovétere, Alberto de la Riva, Enrique Wyld, Carlos García Urrea, Carlos Alfredo Chamier, and René García Mejía (Molina, 1999).

Under the direction of Rubén Morales Monroy, Guatemalan performances have been largely in the vein of popular realism, which depicts the daily life of the middle and lower classes of Guatemala in a realist manner. The Compañía de Arte Dramático de la Universidad Popular is the most well-liked group in Guatemala because of its long existence and its constant adoption of new techniques. Its clear, direct messages are easily understood and appreciated by the Guatemalan public. The most important political writers are Manuel Galich and Hugo Carrillo. The major playwright focusing on Guatemalan customs is María del Carmen Escobar.

Several initiatives to make theater more popular and accessible to the general public took place in the 1960s and 1970s. One initiative was theater for students, in which junior-high and high-school students performed adaptations of literary works. Another measure attempted to bring theater to the interior of the country. Led by Norma Padilla, who found some private sponsorships to carry out the project, an effort was made to send professionals to the different provinces to train those interested in developing theater. Several shows were held in Guatemala City that showcased amateur actors and actresses from the interior. Later these became a minor part of regional festivals that came under the supervision of the minister of culture and sports (Molina, 1999).

One group that formed in Quetzaltenango was *ACSA*, which put on the play "Women of War," written and directed by Fran Lepe. The play features four women of diverse ethnic backgrounds who act out the effects the 36-year war has had on them. Included are representations of the hardships suffered by Mayan women, street urchins, and university students. At the end of the performances, the audience is invited to discuss the play with the director and the actresses.

Some of the theater groups that formed in Guatemala City between the 1960s and 1990s that experimented with different forms of performances were Axial 9-70, Teatrocentro, and Grupo Diez. These groups performed plays at the Grupo Artístcico de Escenificación Moderna (Artistic Group for a Modern Stage), a building that was used exclusively for theater performances from 1960 until it was shut down in 1994. The current principal theater is the Centro Cultural Miguel Angel Asturias (Miguel Angel Asturias Cultural Center), built to take the place of the former Teatro Colón. After other efforts had failed, the building was opened in 1978. Designed by the famous Guatemalan architect Efraín Recinos, it is a fantastic combination of Mayan motifs and contemporary sculptural representations. This majestic architectural wonder is constructed on a lot of eight and a half city blocks. It is one of the largest theaters in Latin America and is larger than most theaters in Europe (see Chapter 8). Outside of Guatemala City the impressive Teatro Municipal Quetzaltenango, inaugurated in 1895, has been the center of theatrical activities in Quetzaltenango for over 100 years.

REFERENCES

Aguirre Beltrán, Gonzalo. *La población negra en México*. México, D.F.: Fondo de Cultura Económica, 1984.
Arrivillaga Cortés, Alfonso. "La música tradicional garífuna en Guatemala." *Latin American Music Review* 11.2 (1990): 251–80.

Centro Cultural Miguel Angel Asturias. Available at http://www.infovia.com.gt/tea-tronacional/historia.htm.

Darer, Monica. "A Birthday Whirl." *Revue* 7.3 (December 1989). Available at http://www.revue.conexion.com/articles/1998/dec/bday.html.

Edmonson, Munroe. *Quiché Dramas and the Divinatory Calendar.* New Orleans, LA: Middle American Research Institute, 1997.

Garcia Escobar, Carlos René. *Atlas danzario de Guatemala.* Guatemala City: Universidad de San Carlos de Guatemala, 1996.

———. "Breves notas sobre las danzas tradicionales de Guatemala." *Folkore Americano* 47 (1989): 71–83.

———. "La danza tradicional del palo volador en Guatemala." *Folklore Americano* 49 (1970): 181–93.

———. *El español: danzas de moros y cristianos en el área central de Guatemala.* Guatemala City: Ministerio de Cultura y Deportes, 1990.

———. "Notas sobre el Baile de Gigantes en Guatemala." *Folklore Americano* 43 (1987): 43–53.

Juarros, Juan Domingo. *Compendio de la historia de la Ciudad de Guatemala.* Guatemala City: Tip. Nacional, 1937.

Lara Figueroa, Celso A., et al. "Historia, etnografía y aplicaciones del baile de toritos: fiesta y bailes de Santo Domingo Xenacoj, departmento de Sacatepéquez, Guatemala." *La Tradición Popular* 44–45 (1983): 1–42.

Molina, Manuel Fernández. "Los años de gestación de un teatro propio, 1900–1944." *Teatro.* Available at http://www.geocities.com/thetropics/Bay/7004/teatro1.html.

———. "El movimiento teatral en Guatemala: 1945–1959." *El movimiento teatral de 1959 en adelante: se da el despegue y se consolida el moviemento teatral.* Available at http://www.geocities.com/thetropics/Bay/7004/teatro1.html.

Monsanto, Carlos. "Guatemala a través de su Marimba." *Latin American Music Review* 3.1 (1982): 60–72.

Ortiz, Fernando. *Los instrumentos de la música afrocubana.* Vol. 1. Havana: Publicaciones de la Dirección de Cultura del Ministerio de Educación, 1952.

Pinto, V[illeda], Hector Abraham. *Moros y cristianos en Chiquimula de la Sierra.* Guatemala City: Ministerio de Educación, 1983.

Porter, Marcie. "The National Symphony Orchestra of Guatemala—1998 Season Begins." *Revue* 7.1 (April 1998). Available at http://www.revue.conexion.com/articles/1998/apr/mus.html.

Prado Bravo, Carlos Humberto, Jorge Efraín de Leon Regil Ruiz, and Francisco José Cajas Ovando, eds. *Teatro Municipal Quetzaltenango: 100 años.* Quetzaltenango: Editorial el Estudiante, 1995.

8

Contemporary Art and Architecture/ Housing

CONTEMPORARY ART in Guatemala has been shaped by a long cultural history with roots in its pre-Columbian heritage, in the clash of cultures with the arrival of the Europeans in the sixteenth century, and in the gradual amalgamation of different cultural traditions throughout the centuries. Although Guatemalan contemporary artists have been deeply influenced by European artistic styles and trends, they tend to represent native and natural elements that make Guatemala unique. They discover their own expressive modes and techniques to depict the cultural heritage of their people. They also symbolically depict the political and social tragedies that have afflicted Guatemalan society, especially this century's tragedies.

The inspiration for modern art in Guatemala can be found in the *modernista* movement at the beginning of the twentieth century, during which various Latin American artists were influenced by European artistic trends such as cubism, abstractionism, and impressionism. In the 1920s artists such as Rafael Rodríguez Padilla, Carlos Valenti and Carlos Mérida combined European vanguardist tendencies with early Mayan cultural components to create social-realist art which was also influenced by the Mexican muralists.

CARLOS MÉRIDA

Carlos Mérida (1891–1984) is considered a precursor of contemporary modern art in Guatemala. Born in Guatemala City, he traveled at a young age with his family to Quetzaltenango in the Quiché region, where he became involved in the study of his first passion, music. From the age of ten to sixteen he learned how to play music and studied music theory and composition. When he began to go deaf from an infection, he decided it would be better to dedicate himself to painting. But in Mérida's later creative works one may still infer the harmony and rhythm of his infatuation with music.

Mérida returned to Guatemala City at the age of eighteen. He enrolled in the newly established Escuela de Bellas Artes (School of Fine Arts) in Guatemala City, which was founded by the Spanish painter Justo De Gandarias. There he met the extremely talented painter Carlos Valenti (1884–1910), who became his inspiration and first teacher. Valenti introduced Mérida to the avant-garde circles that surrounded the Spanish poet and writer Jaime Sabartés, who familiarized the young artists with innovative styles and techniques coming from Europe.

Mérida's friend, Valenti, at first experimented with still life, but he soon turned to expressionistic art. He represented the surrounding environment in often distorted and monstrous forms. The bitterness apparent in these paintings may be attributed to the increasing blindness of Valenti. Refusing to admit defeat, he and the young Mérida set off on a trip to Europe to experience firsthand the artistic world that they had studied. Their main destination was Paris, where they participated in the *tertulias* in the cafes that took place among all kinds of artists, sculptors, poets and musicians. But Valenti's encroaching blindness drove him to desperation, and three months after their arrival in Paris he committed suicide. He was only twenty-six years old.

Mérida, struggling against the depression brought about by the death of his friend and mentor, immersed himself in work and spent the next four years in Europe, learning as much as possible from the European masters. He studied with vanguardist painters such as Modigliani, Kees Van Dongen and Angel de Amarasa. He learned singular techniques from each of them. He also met the Mexican artists Diego Rivera and Roberto Montenegro. More and more, however, he thought about the Mayan legacy of his homeland and the monuments, sculptures, ceramics and paintings left behind by the Mayan ancestors. Upon his return to Guatemala City in 1914, he began to apply the lessons that he had learned in Europe to express the unique, colorful, native element of the Mayas, which was represented in their weavings and household items.

The oppressive dictatorial regime of Manuel Estrada Cabrera forced many artists to flee the country. Mérida left in 1917 to spend two years in New York, where he became friends with the Mexican poet José Juan Tablada. For the most part, however, his interests did not coincide with the artists he met there. So he left for Mexico in 1919, where he met the famous and controversial minister of culture and education, José Vasconcelos, the official responsible for contracting out the painting of the enormous, spectacular murals on the walls of public buildings in Mexico City. Vasconcelos hired Mérida to paint the children's library of the Secretariate of Public Education (a government building). Mérida painted a watercolor version of Little Red Riding Hood, but he felt out of place with the revolutionary ardor that was prevalent in the muralist movement and in Mexico City in general. He was more interested in indigenous folklore and in representing the brilliant colors of Mayan weavings, ancient Mayan symbolism and popular musical motifs. Some of the better known works he created during this time are *Mujeres de Metepec* (Women of Metepec) (1992), *Campesinos* (Peasants) (1924), *Segadores* (Harvesters) (1928) and *Aguadoras* (Water Bearers) (1929). In all of these works the influence of popular Mayan art is apparent, as is the sensation of flowing, rhythmic movement.

Always searching for new approaches, Mérida returned to Paris for two years, where he was influenced by the abstract art of Miró and Klee. His art became more and more abstract, although it still reflected Mayan themes. He later returned to Mexico, again feeling alienated among the muralists. However, although they had little in common stylistically, Mérida identified with the indigenous artistic tradition apparent in the works of one Mexican muralist, Rufino Tamayo. Because he could not return to Guatemala under the dictatorship, Mérida stayed in Mexico and began to paint Mayan figures and profiles, using watercolors or oil. By a stroke of luck, he was offered the chance to lead the School of Dance of the Secretariate of Public Education. During the next three years he was able to illustrate 160 pre-Columbian indigenous dances through lithographs, representing the traditional dress of various groups. He also became more deeply involved in interpreting traditional Mayan art through abstract forms. His famous watercolor painting *El Tigre* (The Tiger), is an example of this approach.

But it is in his paintings of the late 1930s that Mérida believed he had finally found his true style. In an exposition in New York and Mexico in 1939, Mérida exhibited twenty paintings that he considered representative of what the ancient Mayan artists would have produced in modern times. These paintings represent the human in the form of an amoeba, which develops into other themes that represent Mayan sculptures, reliefs and colors. Mérida's series of paintings entitled *Diez invenciones plásticas sobre el tema del amor* (Ten Plastic Inventions on the Theme of Love) is an example of this period in his career.

In 1938 Mérida became interested in surrealism, especially after the visit to Mexico of the master of surrealist art, André Bretón. Mérida's paintings during that period show a surrealist influence that is evident in the symbolic nature of his titles: *Símbolos de sueños insólitos* (Symbols of Unusual Dreams, 1939), *Sueño de un convaleciente* (Dream of a Convalescent) (1939) and *Penas secretas, Anunciación y Fascinación* (Secret Sorrows, Annunciation and Fascination) (1940). During the 1940s Mérida painted a series of canvases called *A través del mundo maya de los dioses y mitos antiguos* (Through the Mayan World of Gods and Ancient Myths), which portrays the symbolic world of the Mayas in geometric and symmetric colors.

In the 1940s, Mérida returned to Guatemala and became involved in blending pre-Columbian cosmogony with geometry and architecture. In the next decade he painted a series of monumental mosaics, murals and reliefs. With Guatemalan sculptors Guillermo Grajeda Mena and Dagoberto Vásquez Castañeda, he embellished the fronts of the Palacio Municipal in 1956, and of the Instituto Guatemalteco de Seguridad Social in 1959. He also painted huge murals on Mexico's extensive apartment complexes. These works revealed European influences combined with the inspiration of a pre-Columbian Mayan heritage. It is also apparent in such murals as the *Sacerdotes danzantes mayas* (Mayan Priests Dancers), which he painted on the walls of the Bank of Guatemala in 1968.

It has been lamented that many of Mérida's works were sold and became part of private collections, so it is difficult to view his complete works. The lack of attention he has received internationally may be attributed to this. However, he is widely recognized in Guatemala as a major artist and has influenced many important artists.

The Flourishing of the Arts during the Ten Years of Spring

After World War II, Guatemala went through a period that has been called the Ten Years of Spring. This was due to the rule of two democratic, socialist presidents, Juan José Arévalo and Jacobo Arbenz Guzmán. From 1945 to 1954 a new atmosphere that encouraged freedom of expression led to a flourishing of the arts. Various schools and associations of artists and writers were established. The University of San Carlos in Guatemala was granted autonomy, and the School of Humanities, the School of Architecture, the Institute of Anthropology and History, the Indigenous Studies Institute, the Guatemalan Choir, the National Symphony Orchestra of Guatemala and the School of Dance and Theater were all founded. Some of the groups that organized were the Association of Fine Arts Professors and Students, the Guatemalan Association of Revolutionary Artists and Writers, the Saker-ti Group of Young Artists and Writers, and the Society for Musical Arts (Diaz,

1997). These artists were influenced by the generation of the 1930s that had been suppressed by the dictatorships of Estrada Cabrera and Ubico. Los Tepeus was an ethnically diverse, nationalist, Indo-American group that united in the 1940s, along with other populist, folkloric or politically militant groups, to espouse antifascist and anti-imperialist discourse. A group of intellectuals called Acento Group, otherwise known as the Generation of the 40s, emerged from these militant positions. It was with the Generation of the 40s that Guatemalan art came out out of isolation and broke with a scholastic tradition. It began exploring its popular, varied cultural components.

Some of the representative artists of this period were Guillermo Grajeda-Mena, Juan Antonio Franco, Juan Jacobo Rodríguez and Roberto Ossaye. Two important painters and sculptors with near-opposing styles emerged from this generation. One was Roberto González Goyri, whose works reflect the influence of abstract tendencies and who had a profound impact on the unfolding of contemporary art in Central America. The other was Dagoberto Vásquez Castañeda, who was influenced both by the events taking place in his country and by the Mexican muralist movement. He tended more toward a social-realist style. Both of these artists combined their artistic and architectural talents to design murals on the walls of public buildings in Guatemala City. These murals represent the stages of Guatemalan history from the Spanish Conquest to the events after World War II.

CONTEMPORARY ARTISTS

At the end of the Ten Years of Spring in 1954, and with the reestablishment of the dictatorial system under U.S.-supported Colonel Castillo Armas, the first period of modern art ended in Guatemala. But it had planted the seeds for a new movement in the 1950s and 1960s that was revitalized by international events, including the Cuban Revolution. Many artists had studied at the School of Visual Arts (formerly the Fine Arts Academy), and they continued to do so after it reopened later in 1954. They became known as the Second Avant-Garde, and they were deeply influenced by Western artistic tendencies of the 1950s and 1960s. Representative artists of this period are Rodolfo Abularach, Margarita Arzudia, Roberto Cabrera, Elmar Rojas, Luis Díaz, Marco Augusto Quiroa and the multifaceted Efraín Recinos.

Rodolfo Abularach used surrealism and figuration to revitalize traditional Mesoamerican themes. He studied art in Mexico, New York and Guatemala, and he experimented with different forms of abstractions. Drawing became his favorite art form because it allowed him to explore light and dark contrasts, which were of special interest to him. He received two Guggenheim fellowships to study in the United States and moved there in 1960. He is internationally known for his drawings of eyes, which at times take up the entire canvas.

Margarita Arzudia used an abstract-geometric formalism to express ancient, indigenous cultural meanings during the 1960s and 1970s. After moving to Europe in the 1970s, she experimented with sculptural and pictorial designs. She also created art books of poetry. The sculptural paintings she created between 1971 and 1974, called *Homage to Guatemala*, are rich in indigenous symbols and rituals. They feature creatures from the natural world, such as quetzals, monkeys, tigers and crocodiles. She continues to depict images from myths and belief systems that combine the old and the new in her current works.

Roberto Cabrera was deeply influenced by the Mayan-*mestizo* themes depicted in Carlos Mérida's paintings. He spent years doing anthropological field work on the Mayan and Ladino multicultural realities of Guatemala. In the 1960s he drew and painted a series of works that represented indigenous cultural expressions, such as the *Popol Vuh, Maximón*, and the *Characters and Gods of the Chilam-Balam*. In the 1970s he became recognized as a socially committed painter who depicted the issue of military violence at a national and international level. Vértebra, the group he founded with abstract artists Marco Augusto Quiroa and Elmar Rojas in 1969, was based on the importance of sociopolitical realities in art, as opposed to what they considered the frivolous art forms and motifs of the U.S.-dominant cultural values in the United States and Latin America. Vértebra had a significant impact on Central American musicians, writers and painters until it disbanded in 1971.

Elmar Rojas has been associated with magical realism, which became renowned through the novels of the Columbian writer Gabriel García Márquez in the 1960s. Influenced by other Latin American artists such as Ossaye, Abulurach, and Tamayo, Rojas portrayed the social realities of Latin America through fantastic images in elaborate paintings that were densely rich in colors. One painting that demonstrates his concern with the sociopolitical realities of his country is *Los Fusilados* (The Executed) (1970). His later paintings drift away from social commentary and are surreal or archetypal depictions of objects, animals and human forms.

Luis Díaz gained much of his technical knowledge while working for the General Board of Highways as a youth. He later studied for two years at the School of Architecture and then worked as an artistic consultant for an architecture firm. He haunted the National School of Visual Arts without ever formally enrolling. He was inspired to produce what he refers to as "environmental montages" (Diaz, 1997). Marked by these experiences, his style tends toward a geometric abstractionism with sociopolitical commentary. His postmodern *Guatebalas* (Guatebullets), a statement on the violence that dominated Guatemala during the 1970s, won the prize of the Central American Biennial Exhibit in 1971.

Marco Augusto Quiroa, who was influenced by Mérida and the Mexican muralists and folk art, first developed a style that was rich in indigenous Mayan folklore. Some of his paintings of the 1950s that reflect the influence of Mérida and Rufine Tamayo are *Terror Cósmico* (Cosmic Terror) and *Músicas Dormidas* (Sleeping Music). Later he produced works that developed along the lines of geometric abstractionism by applying the radiant colors of Mayan weavings. His sarcasm and fun-loving streak are apparent in his painting and in his writing. He is the author of numerous short stories and novels.

Efraín Recinos combines his training as an engineer and architect with his natural artistic talent as a painter and sculptor. He decorates the walls and buildings of Guatemala City with hallucinatory murals, and creates unique structural wonders in public spaces. He was born in Quetzaltenango in 1928 in the heart of the Quiché region. At the age of four Recinos moved to Guatemala City, where he spent the next eight years educating himself at home. He pursued a formal education that culminated with an engineering degree from the University of San Carlos. At an early age Recinos began to draw fantastic pictures that were populated by exotic creatures, which later became incorporated into his murals and sculptures with images from Mayan, European, Latin American and cosmic worlds. During the 1950s his architectural designs influenced the returning Guatemalan architects who were involved in building and designing public buildings in Guatemala City; this is thought to be the beginning of modern architecture in Guatemala. His artistic and architectural works during the 1960s demonstrated his ability to combine mural paintings and architectural sculptures with Mayan and Spanish Colonial motifs. His ability to integrate baroque, delirious spaces and distinct art forms are apparent in the murals and sculptures that adorn the National Library, the Industrial Park, the Aurora International Airport, the National Theater and many other locations. His astounding architectural masterpiece, which he worked on for sixteen years, is the Miguel Angel Asturias Cultural Center, which houses the Open Air Theater and the Grand Theater. Many of Recinos' works reveal a humorous, joyful, frolicsome personality. They also supply lighthearted critical commentary. His visually impressive sculpture *Música Grande* (Grand Music) (1970) is constructed of marimba and tank parts, offering a critique of war. He states that in his sculptural architecture, he is "anti-rationalist and anti-internationalist" (Diaz, 1997). Recinos has had a major impact on visually redefining Guatemala City, which has become known to some as the "Recinos Museum" (Rama, 1972).

Two artists who reflect different trends than the previous group did are Magda Eunice Sánchez and Joyce Vourvoulias. Sánchez makes a conscious effort to break with academicism. Her nonconformist paintings are of a figurative expressionistic nature. They feature deformed, fantastic and intangible figures that evoke reactions in the spectator. Vourvoulias paints in the mode of geometric abstractionism. A younger generation of artists is now emerging with a postmodern perspective that will open the doors for innovative artistic trends in Guatemala in the new millennium (Díaz, 1997).

ARCHITECTURE

Colonial-style architecture in Guatemala came into being with the construction of Guatemala's first capital in its second site, Ciudad Vieja, after Pedro de Alvarado's conquest of Guatemala in 1524. At first rudimentary, architecture later became more refined with the arrival of trained architects from Spain, who used native craftsmen to construct the edifices. These Mayan craftsmen added their own mark while working on churches, monasteries, convents and forts. Signs of native handiwork are apparent in many of the ruins or the still-standing constructions.

As in other areas the principal municipal buildings were initially constructed with defensive purposes in mind. These crude structures became more sophisticated with time as the influence of the Spanish baroque's ostentatious, ornamental style was felt. However, some plain, large forms persisted. The facades of cathedrals were adorned with malleable stucco materials that were easily molded or sculpted into elaborate geometric, animal or vegetable forms. The highly decorative period of the *churrigueresque* (ultrabaroque) affected colonial architecture, especially during the eighteenth century. It was principally in these decorative tasks, which were left in the hands of native artisans, that Mayan themes manifested themselves.

The numerous earthquakes and volcanic eruptions that repeatedly destroyed the nascent capital of Ciudad Vieja and Antigua were major factors that influenced Guatemalan architecture. As a result, most construction in the area was eventually limited to creating one-story structures with broad, solid foundations that were intended to withstand seismic activities. But in 1773, after Antigua was again destroyed by earthquakes, the capital was transferred to a more stable area. For this reason the surviving colonial architecture of Antigua reflects the Spanish baroque character that was in vogue before the city lost its status as the capital.

The construction of the new capital of Guatemala took place during the late eighteenth and early nineteenth centuries, when French, neoclassic, purist tendencies were emerging. However, the baroque influence continued to manifest itself in the new edifices. As this capital city was born because of the destruction of its previous site, the construction of churches, forts and other buildings emphasized squat, massive structures with thick walls and low towers. Today, whereas Antigua's architecture is viewed as a Spanish baroque style, Guatemala City's architecture is considered predominantly neoclassic.

After the destruction of the new capital by earthquakes in 1918, the reconstruction was undertaken with the influence of the highly decorative art nouveau. Adorned doorways, decorated windows and ornamental stucco designs characterize this trend, which was short-lived in Guatemala. In the 1930s a new preoccupation with the indigenous past was reflected in architectural creations that combined baroque elements, with twisting, curving lines, with native archeological motifs. But it was during the Ten Years of Spring, when numerous exiled Guatemalan artists returned, that Guatemalan architecture flourished in a more international, aesthetic vein. Carlos Mérida was instrumental in integrating mural art with architecture. There were other, influential artists who were associated with the new School of Architecture that opened in the National University. They included Guillermo Grajeda-Mena, Roberto González Goyri, Dagoberto Vásquez and Efraín Recinos. Together they created the Civic Center, an extraordinary construction that combined the architectural, artistic and sculptural talents of these artists. The Palacio Municipal (Municipal Palace), designed by architects Roberto Aycinema and Pelayo Llarena Murua, features an impressive mosaic by Mérida on the inside with murals by Vásquez and Mena on the outside. The Instituto Guatemalteco de Seguridad Social (Social Security Building), designed by Roberto Aycinema Echeverría and Jorge Montes Córdoba, displays an extraordinary relief mural by Goyri.

Due to the turbulent political and economic times of the late 1970s and early 1980s, architectural production in Guatemala practically shut down. But it was reborn in 1986 with new dynamic experiments that were influenced by international trends, such as the use of technology and the emergence of environmental architecture. Numerous buildings and shopping centers throughout the city reflect the new trends that integrate postmodern expressions with pre-Columbian and colonial motifs (Cantero, 1997).

HOUSING

Although there are numerous variations, traditional housing in Guatemala may be divided into the colonial-style homes in the cities and the rural dwellings of the Mayas in the highlands. The former originated with the arrival of the Spaniards, who constructed their houses by imitating those of their homeland, which were deeply influenced by Moorish architectural designs. The temperate climate of Guatemala's first capital was conducive to open-air designs, and interior open-air patios with fountains and gardens were essential features. One entered the house through an doorway that led to an open-air patio surrounded by roofed corridors, which connected into the numerous enclosed rooms. The principal rooms of the house, the kitchen, living and dining rooms and bedrooms, looked out into the patio. Some homes had a separate room that functioned as an oratory. The sound of the fountain in the patio permeated this area.

These colonial-style homes had servants' quarters that faced into a smaller patio. The servants' quarters contained a pantry, a kitchen with large chimneys, an oven and an area to eat. The *pilas*, which were large, stone constructions that were filled with water to wash clothes and cookware, were also in this secondary patio. In the wealthier homes, a third patio functioned as a corral, which was an area to grow fruit trees and vegetables, a stable for horses or other beasts of burden and sanitary facilities.

After the first earthquake that destroyed Ciudad Vieja, care was taken to construct only one-story homes, although some contained a higher balcony that overlooked the city. These balconies were carefully constructed with stone and iron. The entranceways and wooden doors were designed with bronze and iron. The doors included heavy knockers of the same materials.

The interiors of the homes were generally simple, with clay-brick floors, whitewashed walls and wooden ceilings. Baths were designed with blue tiles and decorated with stucco ornaments through which the water flowed. Furniture was basic. Sofas and comfortable chairs were in the living room. Beds, often with canopies, wardrobes and cabinets were in the bedrooms. A table and chairs were in the dining room. Paintings were mostly of a religious nature.

As time passed many of these homes were modified to fit economic necessities, but this colonial-style housing is still common in Antigua and may be found in other Guatemalan cities.

Rural housing originated in pre-Columbian times and continues today in modified forms. It makes use of the natural materials locally available. In the higher regions, straw and tile are used for roofs. In the lower areas, roofs consist of palm, sugarcane and cane leaves. In recent years tin or laminated zinc panels serve as roofs, detracting from the natural beauty of rural villages and towns. Walls are constructed principally with cane or adobe. After the earthquake of 1976, however, concrete became the preferred material.

Generally, there is one room that is divided into a kitchen and sleeping areas by the use of cane dividers or *petates* (woven cane or straw mats). The floors are dirt, and people sleep on their *petates*. Because of a lack of electricity and scarce windows in many areas, the rooms are usually dark. At times and if affordable, the kitchen may be a separate, nearby construction. There is very little furniture. There may be a couple of chairs or a bench and sometimes a table. Most homes have some kind of chest in which to store valuables, such as *huipiles* intended for future sale. But no matter how impoverished, every home contains some kind of altar that venerates popular saints.

The outside area consists of a small plot of land that is usually enclosed by cane fences. The land is used to grow fruits and vegetables and to keep chickens, pigs or other small farm animals. An outdoor, covered area next to the home functions as a place to greet visitors, eat meals or sit and weave. Most homes are guarded by one or more mixed-breed dogs that loudly announce visitors and seem to have uncanny abilities for survival on the generally meager provisions that they receive. Usually there are no bathrooms in the modern sense. Rather, there is an area separate from the house with a hole in the ground, or the natural surroundings are used. *Tamascales* are stone constructions with clay roofs that function as vapor baths in certain areas.

Forms of housing in the large urban centers, especially Guatemala City, range from elegant, colonial-style homes to middle-class, Western-style housing to the shantytowns that have sprung up like mushrooms as hundreds of thousands of displaced Mayas and impoverished Ladinos have flocked to the cities looking for a means of survival. The visitor flying into Guatemala City is at first mesmerized by the imposing, haunting nearby volcanoes. Then one is struck by the contrast with the miles and miles of unsightly tin-roofed shacks that function as housing for thousands on the outskirts of the city.

As Guatemala enters the new millennium it must meet the challenge posed by an increasing urban population, which causes subsequent problems for mass transportation, parking, human congestion and pollution. There are few spaces for parks, playgrounds and other outdoor areas. And there is an enormous urban population living in unsanitary, unsightly shacks that surround the city. There have been some experiments to create low-cost urban and rural housing. These projects need to be expanded and improved in the next century to reflect the creative richness of Guatemalan architecture that is prevalent in the areas and buildings where the upper classes live.

REFERENCES

Cancel, Luis R., et al. *The Latin American Spirit: Art and Artists in the United States, 1920–1970*. New York: Bronx Museum of the Arts/Abrams, 1988.

Cantero, Eduardo Aguirre. *Spaces and Volumes: Contemporary Architecture of Guatemala*. Guatemala City: G&T Foundation and Pisos El Aguila, 1997.

Cardoza y Aragón, Luis. *Carlos Mérida: Color y forma*. Mexico City: Dirección General de Publicaciones, Consejo Nacional para la Cultura y las Artes, 1992.

Díaz, Luis, Luz Méndez de la Vega, Roberto Cabrera Padilla, and Thelma Castillo Jurado, eds. *Guatemala. Arte Contemporáneo*. Guatemala City: G & T Foundation, 1997.

Hernández, Manolo. *Prolegómenos a la historia del arte plástico en Guatemala*. Guatemala City: Ministerio de Educación, 1976.

Luján Muñoz, Luis. *Carlos Mérida, precursor del arte contemporáneo Latinoamericano*. Guatemala City: Cuadernos de la tradición guatemalteca, 1985.

———. *Síntesis de la arquitectura en Guatemala*. Guatemala City: Universidad de San Carlos, 1968.

Markman, David Sidney. *Architecture and Urbanization of Colonial Central America*. Tempe: Arizona State University Center for Latin American Studies, 1993.

Rodas, Ana María. *Efraín Recinos y su obra*. Guatemala City: Fundación PAIZ, 1991.

Rodríguez, Josefina Alsono de, ed. *Arte Contemporáneo. Occidente-Guatemala*. Guatemala City: Universidad de San Carlos, 1966.

Shéleshneva-Solodónikova, Natalia A. "Carlos Mérida: la herencia de los antepasados y la estética de la razón." *América Latina* 12 (1991): 84–92.

Zuñiga, Juan Carlos Flores. *Magic and Realism: Central American Contemporary Art*. Tegucigalpa, Honduras: Ediciones Galería de Arte Trio's, 1992.

Glossary

adelantado. governor

aguardiente. moonshine

atol. corn- or rice-based drink

baile. informal, spontaneous or couple dancing

barriletas. kites

boj. sugarcane drink

borracho. drunkard; also a popular dish made with sugar, cinnamon, flour and rum

buñuelo. fried dumplings in honey

cabañuelas. first twelve days of the year; considered omens for corresponding months of the year

cabildo. town council

caldo. soup

cantina. bar

carne asado. charcoal-broiled filet of beef

chicha. wine made from fruits such as apples, peaches or cherries mixed with cinnamon, sugar and white rum

chicharrones. fried pork rinds

chiles rellenos. stuffed peppers

chojín. type of Guatemalan salad

churrigueresque. ultrabaroque

cofradías. religious brotherhoods that venerate and care for a saint

comadre. godmother

comal. clay platter

combos infantiles. children's musical groups

cometas. kites

compadrazgo. relationship between the family and the godparents of their children

compadre. godfather

copal. incense

cortes. skirts

costumbre. tradition

criollos. men and women of Spanish descent born in Latin America

danza. ritualized, choreographed and rehearsed dance

delantal. apron

encomendero. landowner

encomienda. indentureship

fajas. sashes

fiambre. salad of cold meat and vegetables that is prepared on special holidays

fogatas. fire; luminary used to light the street for processions

gigantes. giants

guacamole. avocado salad

guachibal. individual or familiar practice of worshiping a saint in the privacy of one's home

huehuecho. goiter

huipiles. Maya women's intricately woven and/or embroidered blouses

huisquil. chayote

indigenismo. indigenism

indigenista. indigenist

intendente. intendant; quartermaster general

invierno. winter

jocón. chicken dish

loas. short theatrical pieces originally that were intended to be part of the intermission for full-length plays

luminarias. a votive candle set inside a small, decorative paper bag that is weighted with sand

Mam. grandfather; ancient Mayan deity

marimba. type of wooden xylophone

milpas. small plots of land where families grow their traditional crops and raise their animals

misa del gallo. midnight mass

modernismo. Hispanic modernism at the turn of the nineteenth/twentieth century

modernista. modernist in the Hispanic sense

mole. stew or dessert made with chocolate

muestras. shows

nacimiento. nativity or manger scene

nahuales. animal spirits

novena. nine-day ritual before Christmas

occidente. Western

oriente. Eastern

palo de pito. wooden doll with many whistle holes

pañuelos. square cloth worn on the head

pastorelas. shepherd's song

patín. freshwater minnows cooked with tomatoes and chiles

pepián. chicken gruel

pepitoria. squash seeds

personalismo. system of government in which the friends and family of a politician continue to control the government

petate. woven straw mat

pila. stone washbasins with running water that are set up in neighborhoods for laundry

pinol. chicken-flavored corn gruel

pitos. whistles

pom. incense

posada. shelter

posadas. people who symbolically accompany the Virgin Mary and Joseph in their search for shelter during Christmas festivities

puro. handrolled cigarette

rebozo. shawl

repartimiento. villages populated solely by Indians; created by Spaniards to control the Indian population and appropriate their land

reyes magos. three kings of the Orient

rompopo. a drink made with sweetened condensed milk, egg yolks and rum

servilleta. napkin

seviche. shellfish, shrimp or squid chilled in lemon juice and mixed with tomatoes, onions, mint, parsley and hot chiles

sopa de ajo. soup of garlic and bread

tamales. bits of chicken or pork, corn paste or potatoes steamed in banana leaves or in foil

tamascales. stone constructions with clay roofs that function as vapor baths

tambores. drums

teatro misionero. missionary theater

tertulias. informal discussions about literature or the arts

testimonio. testimonial novel

tienda. local store

tierra caliente. hot, humid region

tierra fría. cold region

tierra templada. temperate region

tortillando. process of making tortillas

traje. traditional Mayan dress

verano. summer

villancicos. lyrical poetry sung in processions or at church about the birth of Jesus

zarzuelas. Spanish musical comedies

Bibliography

Aguirre Beltrán, Gonzalo. *La población negra en México*. México, D.F.: Fondo de Cultura Económica, 1984.

Ak'abal, Humberto. *El animalero* (The Anmimaler). Guatemala City: Ministerio de Cultura y Deportes, 1991.

———. *Guardián de la caída de agua* (The Guardian of the Falling Water). Guatemala City: Serviprensa Centroamericana, 1993.

Alejos García, José. "Naturaleza y Perspectiva de la Cofradía Indígena en Guatemala." *Guatemala Indígena* 17.1–2 (1982): 89–158.

Anglesey, Zoe. *Ixok Amar-Go: Central American Women's Poetry for Peace*. Penobscot, ME: Granite Press, 1987.

Annis, Sheldon. *God and Production in a Guatemalan Town*. Austin: University of Texas Press, 1987.

Arana, Ana. "Attacks on the Press 1995: The Americas." Committee to Protect Journalists Publications Index: CPJ Website, 1996. Available at http://www.cpj.org/pubs/attacks95/att95americas.html.

Arévalo, Teresa. *Rafael Arévalo Martínez: Biografía de 1926 hasta su muerte en 1975*. Guatemala City: Oscar de León Palacios, 1995.

Arévalo Martínez, Rafael. *Los atormentados* (The Tormented Ones). Guatemala City: R. Gutierrez y Compañía, 1914.

———. *El hombre que parecía un caballo* (The Man Who Looked Like a Horse). Quezaltenango, Guatemala: Tip. Arte Nuevo, 1915.

———. *Llama* (Flame). México City: Imprenta Mundial, 1934.

———. *Manuel Aldano*. Guatemala City: Talleres Gutenberg, 1922.

———. *El mundo de los maharachías* (The World of Special Creatures). Guatemala City: Unión Tipográfica, 1939.

———. *Las noches en el palacio de la Nunciatura* (Nights in the Palace of the Nunciatura). Guatemala City: Ministerio de Cultura y Deportes, 1988.

————. *La oficina de paz de Orolandia: Novela del imperialismo yanqui* (The Peace Office of Orolandia: A Novel of Yankee Imperialism). Guatemala City: Sánchez y De Guise, 1925.

————. *Por un caminito asi* (Along that Little Pathway). Guatemala City: Unión Tip., 1947.

————. *Las rosas de Engaddi* (The Roses of Engaddi). Guatemala City: Impr. de M. W. Curthiz, 1921.

————. *El señor Monitot* (Mr. Monitot). N.p: Sánchez y de Guise, 1922.

————. *El trovador colombiano* (The Colombian Trobadour). Quezaltenango, Guatemala: Tip. Arte Nuevo, 1915.

————. *Viaje a Ipanda* (Voyage to Ipanda). Guatemala City: Centro Editorial, 1939.

————. *Una vida* (A Life). Guatemala City: Imprenta Electra, 1914.

Arias, Arturo. *After the bombs*. Willimantic, CT: Curbstone, 1990.

————. *Los caminos de Paxil*. Guatemala City: Ministerio de Cultura y Deportes, 1990.

————. "Conciencia de la palabra: Algunos rasgos de la nueva narrativa centroamericana." *Hispamérica: Revista de Literatura* 61 (April 1992): 41–58.

————. "Descolonizando el conocimiento, reformulando la textualidad: Repensando el papel de la narrativa centroamericana." *Revista de Crítica Literaria Latinoamericana* 21 (1995): 42, 73–86.

————. *Después de las bombas*. Mexico: Joaquín Mortiz, 1979.

————. *Itzam-ná*. La Habana: Casa de las Américas, 1981.

————. *Jaguar en llamas* (Jaguar in Flames). Guatemala City: Ministerio de Cultura y Deportes, 1989.

Arrivillaga Cortés, Alfonso. "La música tradicional garífuna en Guatemala." *Latin American Music Review* 11.2 (1990): 251–80.

Asturias, Miguel Angel. *The Bejeweled Boy* (El alhajadito). Garden City, NY: Doubleday, 1971.

————. *Leyendas de Guatemala* (Legends of Guatemala). Madrid: Ediciones Oriente, 1930.

————. *Men of Maize* (Hombres de maíz). Trans. Gerald Martin. London: Verso, 1988.

————. *Mulata de tal* (The Hybrid Mulatta). New York: Delacorte Press, 1967.

————. *Los ojos de los enterrados* (The Eyes of the Interred). New York: Delacorte Press, 1973.

————. *El papa verde* (The Green Pope). New York: Delacorte Press, 1971.

————. *El Señor Presidente* (Mr. President). New York: Atheneum, 1964.

————. *Viento fuerte* (Strong Wind). New York: Delacorte Press, 1968.

Balcárcel, José Luis. "Literatura y liberación nacional en Guatemala." *Casa de las Américas* 126 (May–June 1981): 17–26.

Barrientos, Alfonso E. *Enrique Gómez Carrillo*. Guatemala City: Editorial José Piñeda Ibarra, 1973.

Bellini, Giuseppe. *La narrativa de Miguel Angel Asturias*. Buenos Aires: Losada, 1969.

Benamou, Catherine. "El Norte." *Cine Si-New Latin American Cinema* (Fall 1984): 26–31.

Beverly, John. "The Real Thing." In George M. Gugelberger, ed., *The Real Thing: Testimonial Discourse and Latin America.* Durham, NC: Duke University Press, 1996.

Beverly, John, and Marc Zimmerman. *Literature and Politics in the Central American Revolutions.* Austin: University of Texas Press, 1990.

Binns, Niall. "Tintin en Hispanoamérica: Augusto Monterroso y los estereotipos del cómic." *Cuadernos Hispanoamericanos* 568 (October 1997): 51–66.

Bogantes, Claudio, and Ursula Kuhlmann. "El surgimiento del realismo social en Centroamérica, 1930–1970." *Revista de Crítica Literaria Latinoamericana* 9.17 (1983): 39–64.

Brockett, Charles D. "Malnutrition, Public Policy, and Agrarian Change in Guatemala." *Journal of Inter-American Studies and World Affairs* 26.4 (1984): 477–97.

Burton, Julianne. *Cinema and Social Change in Latin America: Conversations with Filmmakers.* Austin: University of Texas Press, 1986.

Callan, Richard. *Miguel Angel Asturias.* Boston: Twayne, 1970.

Cancel, Luis R., et al. *The Latin American Spirit: Art and Artists in the United States, 1920–1970.* New York: Bronx Museum of the Arts/Abrams, 1988.

Cantero, Eduardo Aguirre. *Spaces and Volumes: Contemporary Architecture of Guatemala.* Guatemala City: G&T Foundation and Pisos de Aguila, 1997.

Cardona, R. "Descripción de la estructura social y económica en el agro Guatemalteco 1954–1975." *Política y Sociedad* 6 (July–December 1978): 5–43.

Cardoza y Aragón, Luis. *Apolo y Coatlicue. Ensayos mexicanos de espina y flor* (Mexican Essays of Thorns and Flowers). México, D.F.: Ediciones de la Serpiente Emplumada, 1944.

———. *Carlos Mérida: Color y forma.* Mexico City: Dirección General de Publicaciones, Consejo Nacional para la Cultura y las Artes, 1992.

———. *Dibujos de ciego* (Blind Drawings) México, D.F.: Siglo XXI, 1969.

———. *Guatemala, las líneas de su mano* (Guatemala, the Lines of Your Hand). México, D.F.: Fondo de Cultura Económico, 1953.

———. *Luna Park.* Paris: Editorial Excelsior, 1924.

———. *Maelstrom: Films telescopiados* (Telescopic Films). Paris: Excelsior, 1926.

———. *La nube y el reloj* (The Cloud and the Watch), México, D.F.: Ediciones de la Universidad Nacional Autónoma, 1940.

———. *Pequeña sinfonía del Nuevo Mundo* (Small Symphony of the New World). Guatemala City: Ediciones El Libro de Guatemala, 1948.

———. *Poesías completas y algunas prosas* (Complete Poems and Some Prose). México, D.F.: Siglo XXI, 1970.

———. *Quinta estación* (Fifth Season). San José, Costa Rica: Editoral Universitara Centroamericana, 1972.

———. *El sonámbulo* (The Sleepwalker). México, D.F.: Angel Chápero, 1937.

Castañeda Medinilla, José. "¿Cofradía o gobierno tribal?" *Guatemala Indígena* 17.1–2 (1982): 89–95.

———. "Maximón, un caso de magia imitativa." *Guatemala Indígena* 14.3–4 (1979): 131–42.

Castillo, Otto René. *Vámonos patria a caminar* (Let Us Move Forward, Nation). Guatemala City: Ed. Vanguardia, 1965.

Chicas Rendón, Otto, and Héctor Gaitán Alfaro. *Recetario y Oraciones Secretas de Maximón*. Guatemala City: Nueva Guatemala de la Asunción, 1995.

Cohen, Isaac, and Gert Rosenthal. "The Dimensions of Economic Policy Space in Central America." In R. Fagan and O. Pellicer, eds., *The Future of Central America: Policy Choices for the U.S. and Mexico*. Stanford, CA: Stanford University Press, 1983. 15–34.

Craft, Linda. *Novels of Testimony and Resistance from Central America*. Gainesville: University Press of Florida, 1997.

Darer, Monica. "A Birthday Whirl." *Revue* 7.3 (December 1998). Available at http://www.revue.conexion.com/articles/1998/dec/bday/html.

Diaz, Luis, Luz Méndez de la Vega, Roberto Cabrera Padilla, and Thelma Castillo Jurado, eds. *Guatemala. Arte Contemporáneo*. Guatemala City: GT Foundation, 1997.

D'Souza, Dinesh. *Illiberal Education: The Politics of Race and Sex on Campus*. New York: Free Press, 1991.

Esquivel Velásquez, Julia. *The Certainty of Spring: Poems by a Guatemalan in Exile*, trans. Anne Whoerle. Washington, DC: Ecumenical Program on Central America, 1993.

———. *El Padre Nuestro desde Guatemala y otros poemas* (Our Father from Guatemala and Other Poems). San José, Costa Rica: Departamento Ecuménico de Investigaciones, 1981.

Edmonson, Munro S. *Quiché Dramas and Divinatory Calendars*. New Orleans, LA: Middle American Research Institute, 1997.

Ethiel, Nancy. "The Robert R. McCormick Tribune Foundation." *MTF Journalism/ 1994 Annual Report*. Available at http://rrmtt.org/journalism/jchap94.htm.

Falla, Ricardo. "Juan El Gordo: visión indígena de su explotación." *Estudios Centroamericanos* 26.268 (1971): 98–107.

———. *Masacres de la Selva*. Guatemala City: Editorial Universitaria, 1992.

———. *Massacres in the Jungle*. Julia Howland, trans. Boulder, CO: Westview Press, 1994.

Fischer, Edward F., and R. Mckenna Brown, eds. *Maya Cultural Activism*. Austin: University of Texas Press, 1996.

Fitzgerald, Mark. "Unprecedented Independence." *Editor and Publisher* 128.27 (July 1995). Available at www.northernlight.com.

Flores, Marco Antonio. *Los compañeros* (The Comrades). México, D.F.: Joaquín Mortiz, 1976.

Foppa, Alaíde. *Elogio de mi cuerpo: dieciocho poemas* (Eulogy to My Body). México, D.F.: Litoarte, 1970.

———. *Las palabras y el tiempo* (Words and Time). Flushing, NY: La Vida Press, 1979.

Foster, George. "Cofradía y Compadrazgo en España e Hispano-América." *Guatemala Indígena* 1.1 (1961): 107–47.

Fried, Jonathan. "*When the Mountains Tremble.*" *Areito* 9–10 (1983–84): 60–61.

Galich, Manuel. *Del pánico al ataque* (From Panic to Attack). Guatemala City: Editorial Universitaria, 1977.

———. *Guatemala*. Havana, Cuba: Casa de las Américas, 1968.

García Escobar, Carlos René. "Los actuales tiempos y los escritores." *La Hora*, September 12, 1992.

———. *Atlas danzario de Guatemala* (Dance Atlas of Guatemala). Guatemala City: Universidad de San Carlos de Guatemala, 1996.

———. "Breves notas sobre las danzas tradicionales de Guatemala." *Folklore Americano* 47 (1989): 71–83.

———. "La danza tradicional del palo volador en Guatemala." *Folklore Americano* 49 (1970): 181–93.

———. *El español: danzas de moros y cristianos en el área central de Guatemala* (The Spaniard: Dances of Moors and Christians in the Central Area of Guatemala). Guatemala City: Ministerio de Cultura y Deportes, 1990.

———. "Notas sobre el Baile de Gigantes en Guatemala." *Folklore Americano* 43 (1987): 43–53.

Garma, Isabel [Norma García Mainieri]. *Cuentos de muerte y resurreción* (Stories of Death and Resurrection). México, D.F.: Federation Ed. Mexicana, 1987.

Garrard-Burnett, Virginia. *Protestantism in Guatemala: Living in the New Jerusalem.* Austin: University of Texas Press, 1998.

Garzon, Susan, R. Mckenna Brown, Julia Becker Richards, and Wuqu'Ajpub'. *The Life of Our Language.* Austin: University of Texas Press, 1998.

Girón Mena, Manuel Antonio. *Rafael Arévalo Martínez: Su vida y obra* (His Life and Works). Guatemala City: Editorial José de Piñeda Ibarra, 1974.

Goldman, Francisco. *The Long Night of the White Chickens.* New York: Atlantic, 1992.

Gómez Carrillo, Enrique. *El alma encantadora de París* (The Enchanting Soul of Paris). Barcelona: Maucci, 1902.

———. *De Marsella a Tokio: Sensaciones de Egipto, la India, la China y el Japón* (From Marseilles to Tokyo: Sensations of Egypt, India, China and Japan). Paris: Garnier, 1906.

———. *Desfile de visiones* (Parade of Visions). Valencia, 1906.

———. *El encanto de Buenos Aires* (The Enchantment of Buenos Aires). Madrid: Perlado, Páez y Compañía, 1914.

———. *La Grecia eterna* (Eternal Greece). Madrid: Editorial "Mundo Latino," 1920.

————. *El Japón heroico y galante* (Heroic and Gallant Japan). Madrid: Renacimiento, 1912.

————. *La Rusia actual* (Russia Today). Paris: Garnier, 1906.

————. *La sonrisa de la esfinge (Egipto)* (The Smile of the Sphinx). Madrid: Renacimiento, 1913.

————. *Treinta años de mi vida* (Thirty Years of My Life). Madrid: Editorial "Mundo Latino," 1920–1923.

González, Gasper Pedro. *A Mayan Life*. Elaine Elliott, trans. Rancho Palos Verdes, CA: Yax Té Foundation, 1995.

————. *La otra cara* (A Mayan Life). Guatemala City: Editorial Cultura, Ministerio de Cultura y Deportes, 1992.

————. *El retorno de los mayas*. Guatemala City: Fundación Myrna Mack, 1998.

————. *The Return of the Maya*. Susan G. Rascón, trans. Rancho Palos Verdes, CA: Yax Té Foundation, 1998.

Handy, Jim. *Gift of the Devil*. Boston: South End Press, 1984.

Hendrickson, Carol. "Handmade and Thought-Woven: The Construction of Dress and Social Identity in Tecpan Guatemala." Ph.D. diss., University of Chicago, 1986.

————. *Weaving Identities*. Austin: University of Texas Press, 1995.

————. "Women, Weaving and Education in Maya Revitalization." In Edward F. Fischer and R. Mckenna Brown, eds. *Maya Cultural Activism*. Austin: University of Texas Press, 1996. 156–64.

Hernández, Manolo. *Prolegómenos a la historia del arte plástico en Guatemala*. (Prolegomena to the History of Plastic Arts in Guatemala). Guatemala City: Ministerio de Educación, 1976.

Herring, Hubert. *A History of Latin America*. New York: Alfred A. Knopf, 1972.

Hill, Robert M., II. "Manteniendo el culto a los santos: aspectos financieros de las instituciones religiosas en el altiplano colonial maya." *Mesoamérica* 7.11 (1986): 61–77.

Hough, R. *Land and Labor in Guatemala: An Assessment*. Guatemala City: Ediciones Papiro, 1983.

Hurtado, Juan José. "Algunas ideas sobre el culto de los animales y el nahualismo en el siglo XVIII." *Guatemala Indígena* 6.4 (1971): 176–83.

Interiano, Carlos. *Comunicación, periodismo y paz en Guatemala* (Communication, Journalism and Peace in Guatemala). Guatemala City: Universidad de San Carlos, 1996.

International Institute for Democracy and Electoral Assistance. "The Challenge of the Media in Guatemala. Democracy in Guatemala: A Mission for the Entire Nation. Stockholm, Sweden." International IDEA, 1998. Online. April 2000. Available at http://www.int-idea.se/publications/Guatemala/engguat-9media.html.

Jonas, Susan, and David Tobias, eds. *Guatemala*. Berkeley: North American Congress on Latin America, 1974.

Juarros, Juan Domingo. *Compendio de la historia de la Ciudad de Guatemala* (Compendium of the History of Guatemala City). Guatemala City: Tip. Nacional, 1937.

King, John. *Magical Reels: A History of Cinema in Latin America.* London: Verso, 1990.

Krauel, Ricardo. "La república clausurada: análisis de los espacios opresivos en *El señor presidente.*" *Monographic Review/Revista Monográfica,* 11 (1995): 220–34.

Lara Figueroa, Celso A. et al. "Historia, etnografía y aplicaciones del baile de toritos: fiesta y bailes de Santo Domingo Xenacoj, departmento de Sacatepéquez, Guatemala." *La Tradición Popular* 44–45 (1983): 1–42.

Liano, Dante. *La palabra y el sueño* (The Word and the Dream). Rome: Bulzoni Editore, 1984.

Lión Díaz, Luis de. *El tiempo principia en Xibalbá* (Time Begins in Xibalbá). Guatemala City: Ed. Serviprensa Centroamericana, 1985.

Lovell, George. *Conquest and Survival in Colonial Guatemala.* Montreal: McGill-Queen's University Press, 1992.

Luján Muñoz, Luis. *Carlos Mérida, precursor del arte contemporáneo Latinoamericano* (Carlos Mérida: Precursor of Latin American Contemporary Art). Guatemala City: Cuadernos de la tradición guatemalteca, 1985.

———. *Sintesis de la arquitectura en Guatemala* (Synthesis of Guatemalan Architecture). Guatemala City: Universidad de San Carlos, 1968.

———. *Tradiciones navideñas de Guatemala* (Christmas Traditions of Guatemala). Guatemala City: Cuadernos de la Tradición Guatemalteca, 1986.

Macleod, M. J. *Spanish Central America: A Socioeconomic History, 1520–1720.* Berkeley: University of California Press, 1973.

Markman, David Sidney. *Architecture and Urbanization of Colonial Central America.* Tempe, AZ: Arizona State University Center for Latin American Studies, 1993.

Marks, Copeland. *False Tongues and Sunday Bread.* New York: M. Evans and Company, Inc., 1985.

Masoliver, Juan Antonio. "Augusto Monterroso o la tradición subversiva." *Cuadernos Hispanoamericanos* 408 (1984): 146–154.

Meléndez, Ofelia Columba Déleon. *La feria de Jocotenango en la ciudad de Guatemala: una aproximación histórica y etnográfica* (The Fair of Jocotenango in Guatemala City: A Historic and Ethnographic Approach). Guatemala City: Editorial Universitaria, 1983.

Menchú, Rigoberta. *Crossing Borders.* Trans. Ann Wright (from *Rigoberta: La nieta de los mayas*). London: Verso, 1998.

———. *Me llamo Rigoberta Menchú y así me nació la conciencia* (I, Rigoberta Menchú). Elisabeth Burgos-Debray, ed. México, D.F.: Siglo XXI, 1985.

———. *Rigoberta: La nieta de los mayas.* Collaborators Dante Liano and Gianni

Miná. Madrid: Grupo Santillana de Ediciones, S.A./Ediciones El Pais, S.A., 1998.

Mendelson, E. Michael. *Los Escándalos de Maximón* (The Scandals of Maximón). Guatemala City: Seminario de integracón Social Guatemalteca, 1965.

Méndez de la Vega, Luz. *Eva sin Dios* (Eve Without God). Guatemala City: Editorial Marroquín, 1979.

———. *Las voces silenciadas: Poemas feministas* (Silenced Voices: Feminist Poems). Guatemala City: RIN-78, 1985.

Mendoza, Juan Manuel. *Enrique Gómez Carrillo: estudio crítico-biográfico: su vida, su obra, su época* (Critical-Biographical Study: His Life, Works and Times). Guatemala City: Tipografía Nacional, 1946.

Molina, Manuel Fernández. "Los años de gestación de un teatro propio, 1900–1944." *Teatro*. Available at http://www.geocities.com/thetropics/Bay/7004/teatro1.html.

———. "El movimiento teatral de 1959 en adelante: se da el despegue y se consolida el movimiento teatral." Available at http://www.geocities.com/thetropics/Bay7004/teatro1.html.

Mondloch, James. "Sincretismo religioso maya-cristiano en la tradición oral de una comunidad quiché." *Mesoamérica* 3.3 (1982): 107–23.

Monsanto, Carlos. "Guatemala a través de su Marimba." *Latin American Music Review* 3.1 (1982): 60–72.

Monteforte Toledo, Mario. *Centro America: subdesarrollo y dependencia*. México, D.F.: UNAM, 1975.

———. *Donde acaban los caminos* (Where the Paths End). Guatemala City: Ed. Piedra Santa, 1989.

———. *Entre la piedra y la cruz* (Between the Stone and the Cross). Guatemala City: Ed. "El Libro de Guatemala," 1948.

———. *Guatemala. Monografía sociológica* (Guatemala. Sociological Monograph). México, D.F.: UNAM, 1959.

———. *Una manera de morir* (One Way to Die). Barcelona: Plaza y Janes, 1988.

———. *Y llegaron del mar* (And They Arrived from the Sea). México, D.F.: Joaquín Mortiz, 1966.

Montejo, Victor. *The Bird Who Cleans the World*. Wallace Kaufman, trans. Willimantic, CT: Curbstone Press, 1991.

———. *Testimony: Death of a Guatemalan Village*. Victor Perera, trans. Willimantic, CT: Curbstone Press, 1987.

Monterroso, Augusto. *Los buscadores de oro* (The Gold Seekers). Barcelona: Editorial Anagrama, 1993.

———. *Lo demás es silencio* (The Rest Is Silence). México, D.F.: Joaquín Mortiz, 1969.

———. *La letra "e": Fragmento de un diario* (The Letter "E": A Fragment of a Diary). México, D.F.: Ediciones Era, 1987.

———. *Movimiento perpetuo* (Perpetual Motion). México, D.F.: J. Mortiz, 1972.

———. *Obras completas y otros cuentos* (Complete Works and Other Stories). México, D.F.: UNAM, 1959.

———. *La oveja negra y demás fábulas* (The Black Sheep and Other Fables). México, D.F.: Joaquín Mortiz, 1969.

———. *Viaje al centro de la fábula* (Journey to the Center of the Fables). México, D.F.: UNAM, 1981.

Morales, Mario Roberto. *Señores bajo los árboles ó brevísima relación de la destrucción de los indios: testinovela* (Men Under the Trees, or a Very Brief Account of the Destruction of the Indians: Testinovel). Guatemala City: Artemis, 1994.

Nash, June. *In the Eyes of the Ancestors: Belief and Behavior in a Maya Community.* New Haven, CT: Yale University Press, 1970.

Noguerol Jiménez, Francisca. "Textos como 'esquiarlas': Los híbridos genéricos de Augusto Monterroso." *Insula* 618–19 (June–July 1998): 29–32.

Nyrop, Richard T., ed. *Guatemala: A Country Study.* Washington, DC: The American University of Washington, Foreign Area Studies, 1983.

Ortiz, Fernando. *Los instrumentos de la música afrocubana.* Vol. 1. Havana: Publicaciones de la Dirección de Cultura del Ministerio de Educación, 1952.

Otzoy, Irma. "Maya Clothing and Identity." In Edward F. Fischer and R. Mckenna Brown, eds. *Maya Cultural Activism.* Austin: University of Texas Press, 1996: 141–155.

Paige, J. M. *Agrarian Revolution: Social Movements and Export Agriculture in the Underdeveloped World.* New York: Free Press, 1976.

Pan American Health Organization. "Guatemala." *Health in the Americas, 1998 Edition.* Washington, DC: Government Printing Office, 1998. Available at http://www.paho.org/english/country.htm.

Pardo, J. J., Pedro Zamora, and Luis Luján. *Guía de Antigua Guatemala* (Guide to Antigua Guatemala), 3rd ed. Guatemala City: Editorial José de Pineda Ibarra, 1969.

Payeras, Mario. *Los días de la selva: relatos sobre la implantación de las guerrillas populares en el norte del Quiché, 1972–1976* (Days of the Jungle: Accounts About the Implantation of Popular Guerrilla Armies in the North of Quiché). Guatemala City, 1980.

Perera, Victor. *The Cross and the Pear Tree: A Sephardic Journey.* New York: Knopf, 1995.

———. *Rites: A Guatemalan Boyhood.* San Diego: Harcourt, Brace, Jovanovich, 1986.

Pinto, V[illeda], and Hector Abraham. *Moros y cristianos en Chiquimula de la Sierra* (Moors and Christians in Chiquimula of the Mountains). Guatemala City: Ministerio de Educación, 1983.

Prado Bravo, Carlos Humberto, Jorge Efraín de León Regil Ruiz, and Francisco José Cajas Ovando, eds. *Teatro Municipal Quetzaltenango: 100 años* (Municipal Theater of Quetzaltenango: 100 Years). Quetzaltenango: Editorial el Estudiante, 1995.

Prieto, René. *Miguel Angel Asturias' Archaeology of Return*. Cambridge: Cambridge University Press, 1993.

Porter, Marcie. "The National Symphony Orchestra of Guatemala—1998 Season Begins." *Revue* 7.1 (April 1998). Available at http://www.revue.conexion. com/articles/1998/apr/mus.html.

Quintanilla Meza, Carlos Humberto. *La semana santa en Antigua Guatemala*. La Antigua Guatemala: Consejo Nacional para la Protección de La Antigua Guatemala, 1989.

Rama, Angel. *Excelsior*. July 2, 1972. In *Efraín Recinos y su obra* (Efraín Recinos and His Works). Guatemala City: Fundación PAIZ, 1991.

Ranucci, Karen, and Julie Feldman, eds. *A Guide to Latin American, Caribbean, and U.S. Latino-Made Film and Video*. Lanham, MD: The Scarecrow Press, Inc., 1998.

Richards, Julie Becker, and Michael Richards. "Maya Education: A Historical and Contemporary Analysis of Mayan Language Education Policy." In Edward F. Fischer and R. Mckenna Brown, eds. *Maya Cultural Activism*. Austin: University of Texas Press, 1996.

Rock Chapin. "Alux Nahual." Available at http://www.geocities.com/SunsetStrip/ Disco/5906.alux.html. (Rock Chapin is a group of three young individuals who publish a Website about Guatemalan music.)

Rodas, Ana María. *Cuatro esquinas del juego de una muñeca* (Four Corners in the Doll Set). Guatemala City: Litografías Modernas, n.d.

———. *Efrain Recinos y su obra* (Efrain Recinos and His Works). Guatemala City: Fundación PAIZ, 1991.

———. *El fin de los mitos y los sueños* (The End of Myths and Dreams). Guatemala City: Editorial RIN-78, 1984.

———. *Insurrección de Mariana* (Insurrection of Mariana). Guatemala City: Ediciones del Cadejo, 1993.

———. *Poemas de la izquierda erótica* (Poems of the Erotic Left). Guatemala City: Editoral Landívar, 1973.

Rodríguez, Josefina Alonso de, ed. *Arte Contemporáneo. Occidente-Guatemala*. Guatemala City: Universidad de San Carlos, 1966.

Saler, Benson. "Religious Conversion and Self-Aggrandizement: A Guatemala Case." *Practical Anthropology*, 12.3 (May–June 1965): 107–14.

Salwen, Michael B., and Bruce Garrison. *Latin American Journalism*. Hillsdale, NJ: Lawrence Erlbaum Associates, 1991.

Sanchiz Ochoa, Pilar. "Sincretismo de ida y vuelta: el culto de San Simón en Guatemala." *Mesoamérica* 14.26 (1993): 253–66.

Schnitman, Jorge A. *Film Industries in Latin America*. Norwood, NJ: Ablex, 1984.

Shea, Maureen. "Latin American Women and the Oral Tradition: Giving Voice to the Voiceless." *Critique* 34.3 (Spring 1993): 139–54.

———. Oral interviews with various Mayas during the summers of 1988–1993.

———. "*When the Mountains Tremble* and *I, Rigoberta Menchú*: Documentary Film and Testimonial Literature in Latin America." *Film Criticism* 18.2 (Winter 1994): 3–14.

Shéleshneva-Solodonikova, Natalia A. "Carlos Mérida: la herencia de los antepasados y la estética de la razón." *América Latina* 12 (1991): 84–92.

Smeets, Marylene. "Speaking Out: Postwar Journalism in Guatemala and El Salvador." Committee to Protect Journalists Publication Index. Available at http://www.cpj.org/dangerous/spring99/guatemala11august99.html.

Smith, Carol. *Guatemalan Indians and the State: 1540 to 1988*. Austin: University of Texas Press, 1990.

Smith, Kenneth W. "Todos los Santos: Spirits, Kites, and Courtship in the Guatemalan Maya Highlands." *Folklore Americano* 26 (1978): 49–58.

"Spanish Colonial Art and Architecture." *The Columbia Encyclopedia*, 6th ed. New York: Columbia University Press, 2000. Also available at http://www.bartelby.com/65/sp/spancolo.html.

Sperlich, Norbert, and Elizabeth Katz Sperlich. *Guatemalan Backstrap Weaving*. Norman: University of Oklahoma Press, 1980.

Stavans, Ilan. "On Brevity: A Conversation with Augusto Monterroso." *Massachusetts Review* 37.3 (1996): 393–403.

Stoll, David. *Rigoberta Menchú and the Story of All Poor Guatemalans*. Boulder, CO: Westview Press, 1999.

Tedlock, Dennis, trans. *Popol Vuh*. New York: Simon & Schuster, 1985.

Thomas, David. "The Silence of Neto/El Silencio de Neto." November 7, 1999. Available at http://members.aol.com/tikalan/index.html.

Thompson, Donald E. *Mayan Paganism and Christianity: A History of the Fusion of Two Religions*. New Orleans, LA: Middle American Research Institute, 1954.

Tortolani, Paul. "Political Participation of Native and Foreign Catholic Clergy in Guatemala." *Journal of Church and State*, 15.3 (1973): 407–18.

Villatoro, Eduardo P., and Marco Tulio Barrios Reina, et al. *Comisión de Libertad de Prensa de la Asociación de Periodistas de Guatemala, Report on Press Freedom*. Guatemala City: Inter-American Commission on Human Rights. Organization of American States, August 10, 1998. Available at http://www.ifex.org/alert.00003535.html.

Warren, Kay. *The Symbolism of Subordination*. Austin: University of Texas Press, 1989.

Watanabe, John M. *Maya Saints and Souls in a Changing World*. Austin: University of Texas Press, 1992.

Wilentz, Gay. *Binding Cultures*. Bloomington: Indiana University Press, 1992.

Wolf, Eric R. "Closed Corporate Peasant Communities in Mesoamerica and Central Java." *Southwestern Journal of Anthropology* 13.1 (1957): 1–18.

World Bank. *Guatemala: Economic and Social Position and Prospects*. Washington, DC: Brockett, 1978.

World Health Organization. "Guatemala." WHO Global Database on Child Growth and Malnutrition. Online. July 8, 1999. Available at http://www.who.int/nutgrowthdb.

Zimmerman, Marc. *Literature and Resistance in Guatemala.* Athens: Ohio University Press, 1995.

————. "Testimonios in Guatemala: Payeras, Rigoberta, and Beyond." *Latin American Perspectives* 18 (Fall 1991): 22–47.

Zuñiga, Juan Carlos Flores. *Magic and Realism: Central American Contemporary Art.* Tegucigalpa, Honduras: Ediciones Galería de Arte Trio's, 1992.

Index

About the Author

MAUREEN E. SHEA is Associate Professor of Spanish, Department of Spanish and Portuguese, Tulane University, New Orleans, Louisiana. She is also affiliated with the Latin American Studies and the Women's Studies programs. She has published frequently on Central American literature and Latin American women writers and is the author of *Women as Outsiders: Undercurrents of Oppression in Latin American Women's Novels* (1993).